T0312301

Cambridge Elements ≡

Elements on Women in the History of Philosophy
edited by
Jacqueline Broad
Monash University

PYTHAGOREAN WOMEN

Caterina Pellò
*University College London
and Harvard Center for Hellenic Studies*

CAMBRIDGE
UNIVERSITY PRESS

CAMBRIDGE
UNIVERSITY PRESS

University Printing House, Cambridge CB2 8BS, United Kingdom

One Liberty Plaza, 20th Floor, New York, NY 10006, USA

477 Williamstown Road, Port Melbourne, VIC 3207, Australia

314–321, 3rd Floor, Plot 3, Splendor Forum, Jasola District Centre, New Delhi – 110025, India

103 Penang Road, #05–06/07, Visioncrest Commercial, Singapore 238467

Cambridge University Press is part of the University of Cambridge.

It furthers the University's mission by disseminating knowledge in the pursuit of education, learning, and research at the highest international levels of excellence.

www.cambridge.org
Information on this title: www.cambridge.org/9781009011815
DOI: 10.1017/9781009026864

© Caterina Pellò 2022

First published 2022

A catalogue record for this publication is available from the British Library.

ISBN 978-1-009-01181-5 Paperback
ISSN 2634-4645 (online)
ISSN 2634-4637 (print)

Pythagorean Women

Elements on Women in the History of Philosophy

DOI: 10.1017/9781009026864
First published online: July 2022

Caterina Pellò
University College London and Harvard Center for Hellenic Studies

Author for correspondence: Caterina Pellò, c.pello@ucl.ac.uk

Abstract: The Pythagorean women are a group of female philosophers who were followers of Pythagoras and are credited with authoring a series of letters and treatises. In both stages of the history of Pythagoreanism – namely, the 5th-century Pythagorean societies and the Hellenistic Pythagorean writings – the Pythagorean woman is viewed as an intellectual, a thinker, a teacher, and a philosopher. The purpose of this Element is to answer the question: what kind of philosopher is the Pythagorean woman? The traditional picture of the Pythagorean female sage is that of an expert of the household. The author argues that the available evidence is more complex and conveys the idea of the Pythagorean woman as both an expert on the female sphere and a well-rounded thinker philosophising about the principles of the cosmos, human society, the immortality of the soul, numbers, and harmonics.

Keywords: Pythagorean women, Pythagoreanism, Pythagorean pseudepigrapha, Theano, Perictione

ISBNs: 9781009011815 (PB), 9781009026864 (OC)
ISSNs: 2634-4645 (online), 2634-4637 (print)

Contents

1 Introduction: The Pythagorean Female Sage

The Pythagorean women are a group of female intellectuals who were followers of Pythagoras and are credited with formulating moral precepts and authoring a series of letters and treatises. The evidence for these thinkers ranges from fragmentary materials about Pythagoras educating women in the 5th century BCE in Magna Graecia to a tradition of writings that extends into the 2nd century CE in Alexandria and Rome and was handed down to us as authored by Pythagorean women. Since their attribution has long been debated, these texts are referred to as 'Pythagorean pseudepigrapha'.[1] Therefore, as Nancy Demand writes, in the obscure history of ancient women philosophers, the case of the Pythagoreans 'appears as a comparatively bright spot' (1982: 135). Specifically, the Pythagoreans have attracted the attention of scholars working on women in the history of philosophy for two reasons: first, this is the earliest documented case of female engagement with Greek philosophy. Second, the pseudepigrapha are the first example of philosophical prose ascribed to female authors in Greek antiquity.

This Element introduces readers to the study of the Pythagorean women by reviewing the key questions, sources, scholarly approaches, and challenges and offering new insight into these women's ideas and the contributions of their alleged writings to the history of philosophy. The purpose is to answer the question: what kind of philosopher is the Pythagorean woman?

Like the rest of Pythagoreans,[2] the Pythagorean women are a multifaceted group of thinkers that presents the researcher with a variety of challenges. The writings are conceptually heterogeneous, written in different dialects, and cover a long span of time over the course of four centuries.[3] This fragmentary evidence and pseudepigraphic texts, nonetheless, jointly sketch the picture of the Pythagorean woman as an authoritative teacher and a wise philosopher. The traditional image of the Pythagorean female sage is that of an expert of the household: Pythagoras was known for educating women on how to be faithful wives, nurturing mothers, and devoted daughters, and in turn, the Pythagorean

---

[1] Different scholars have used different names to refer to these Hellenistic and post-Hellenistic writings. Thom calls them 'Neo-Pythagoreans' to distinguish this tradition from early Pythagoreanism (2008: 67–8). By contrast, Reale describes them as 'Middle Pythagoreans' to separate the pseudepigrapha from the other Neopythagorean philosophers (1990: 251–72). Finally, most scholars identify these writings as 'Pseudo-Pythagorean' to highlight the discontinuities from the early Pythagorean tradition (e.g., Centrone, 1990; Zhmud, 2019). I refer to these texts as Pythagorean pseudepigrapha to emphasise that they were not written by the named author but leave open the question of their connection to ancient Pythagoreanism (see also Horky, 2015).

[2] On the many facets of the Pythagorean tradition and Pythagorean scholarship, see Cornelli (2013).

[3] The exact dating of these writings is also debated. For a discussion of this issue, see Section 3.1.1.

women show their pupils how to interact with their husbands and raise their children and are credited with writing letters and treatises about family life and domesticity. Yet I argue that the available evidence is more complex and layered and conveys the idea of the Pythagorean woman as both an expert on the female sphere and a well-rounded thinker. It should be noted that in our ancient sources, the Pythagorean women are rarely referred to as philosophers.[4] What I hope to show, nonetheless, is that the texts ascribed to Pythagorean women often engage in an explanatory, systematic, critical, coherent, unconventional, and argumentative way with key problems in ancient Greek philosophy. Therefore, I use the term 'philosophers' to stress the philosophical nature of their questions and answers.

There are two fundamental difficulties with studying the Pythagorean women and the writings that are attributed to them: the source problem and the pseudonymity issue. On the one hand, the evidence for the role of women in 5th-century Pythagorean societies is limited, and the few surviving sources are fragmentary and of dubious reliability. On the other hand, a large corpus of texts written under the names of Pythagorean women starts to circulate in the 3rd century BCE. The second challenge, then, is not the lack but the *nature* of the evidence. Specifically, scholars have questioned both whether the texts are apocryphal (i.e., not written by the named authors), if they are in fact authored by women or rather by men writing under female pseudonyms, and whether they are of any philosophical value.

In the first part of the Element, I address the first problem and examine the limited, but nonetheless significant, evidence for women in early Pythagorean societies. Our sources show that women are part of Pythagoras' audiences and members of his intellectual circles. Although the available evidence mainly refers to the Pythagorean women as mothers, wives, and daughters of Pythagorean men, some women are also known for excelling at the Pythagorean way of life beyond domesticity. Other women, such as Pythagoras' alleged wife Theano, are said to be educators and lecture their fellow Pythagoreans on a variety of topics, including but not limited to family roles and relationships. In the second part of the Element, I turn to the Pythagorean pseudepigrapha of the Hellenistic period. While I devote a section to reviewing the authorship and pseudonymity debate (Section 3.1.2), I am only secondarily concerned with the question of who wrote the letters and treatises ascribed to Pythagorean women and, most importantly, whether the authors are women. I am first interested in what these texts can tell us about the reception of the Pythagorean women as philosophers. I shall focus on

---

[4] Among the few exceptions is a comment by Clement of Alexandria (*Strom.* 1.80.4) discussed in Section 2.2.3, according to which Pythagoras' wife is the first woman philosopher.

two groups of treatises – the ethical and the theoretical treatises – which take two different paths to argue for women's philosophical potential by depicting their authors, respectively, as female ethicists and as metaphysicians.

Overall, in antiquity and in the various stages of the history of Pythagoreanism, the Pythagorean woman is viewed as an intellectual, a thinker, a teacher, and a philosopher. Specifically, I argue, she is viewed both as an expert of the household and as an all-round sage philosophising about the principles and functioning of the cosmos, human society, the immortality of the soul, numbers, and harmonics. The Pythagorean woman is an authority for women, but she also specialises in embryology, psychology, music theory, eschatology, social and political advice, metaphysics, epistemology, and ethics.

1.1 A Short History of Pythagoreanism

I begin by distinguishing two stages in the history of Pythagoreanism: the early Pythagorean societies, which were founded in Southern Italy in the late 6th century BCE and prospered until the first half of the 4th century,[5] and the revival of Pythagoreanism between the 3rd century BCE and the 3rd century CE. Pythagoras and the other early Pythagoreans, with few exceptions, left no written works.[6] Later sources, nonetheless, describe Pythagoras as a mathematician, an expert on the afterlife and the transmigration of souls, and the founder of a strict way of life for his community of followers. According to Aristotle, some Pythagoreans believed that numbers are the principles of all things and the whole cosmos is structured according to numerical relationships. According to Herodotus, Pythagoras taught that at death, the soul reincarnated in another animal or human body. Finally, according to Plato, the Pythagoreans adhered to a rigorous lifestyle and dietary restrictions in accordance with their ethical and religious beliefs.[7]

In contrast, the Hellenistic and post-Hellenistic periods witness the flourishing of Pythagorean texts. This stage is characterised by a tendency to view Pythagoras as the primary source of influence for later Greek philosophical traditions, such as Platonism, Stoicism, and Aristotelianism. This renewed interest in Pythagoreanism manifests itself in two ways: on the one hand, we find the Neopythagorean philosophers, such as Nigidius Figulus in the 1st

---

[5] On the fall of the early Pythagorean societies, see Aristoxenus Frs. 18–19 (Wehrli, 1974); D.L. 8.46; Iamb. *VP* 251, 265–6. For an analysis of early Pythagorean societies, see von Fritz (1940); Minar (1942); Burkert (1982); Zhmud (2012a: 141–7).

[6] Philolaus of Croton is reputed to be the first Pythagorean to leave a written record of his doctrines (D.L. 8.85; Iamb. *VP* 199).

[7] See Ar. *Met.* 1.5.985b23–24; Hdt. 2.123; Pl. *Rep.* 10.600a–b. The early Pythagorean doctrines are discussed further in Section 2.1.

century BCE in Rome; Apollonius of Tyana in the 1st century CE; and the 2nd-century Platonists Moderatus of Gades, Nicomachus of Gerasa and Numenius of Apamea, all of whom write under their own names about the ancient Pythagorean way of life, mathematics, and metaphysics. On the other, we find the authors of Pythagorean pseudepigrapha, who forge apocryphal writings under the pseudonyms of early Pythagorean philosophers.[8] This corpus comprises treatises, sayings, poems, and letters concerning epistemology, cosmology, metaphysics, logic, and moral and political philosophies; written in various dialects; and surviving either in full or in long fragments. The purpose is again to merge Pythagoreanism with later traditions and depict Pythagoras as the forefather of Platonic and Aristotelian philosophies.

The Pythagorean women, too, are divided into two groups: the early Pythagorean women of the Archaic and Classical Age, and the late, or pseudo, Pythagorean authors of the Hellenistic and Imperial Age. According to the surviving sources, which I discuss later, the early Pythagorean women live around the 5th century BCE in Southern Italy and mainland Greece and are members of Pythagorean societies. Iamblichus lists the names of Pythagoras' seventeen most famous female disciples: Timycha, Philtys, the sisters Occelo and Eccelo, Cratesicleia, Cheilonis, Theano, Myia, Lastheneia, Habroteleia, Echekrateia, Tyrsenis, Peisirrhode, Theadusa, Boeo, Babelyca, and Cleaichma. Some of them are reputed to be members of Pythagoras' own family, such as his wife Theano and his daughter Myia. No direct evidence from this first group of women has been handed down to us. In contrast, the late, and arguably pseudo, Pythagorean women are credited with authoring a comparatively large number of texts. The approximate dating ranges from the 1st century BCE to the 2nd century CE. Once again, the linguistic style suggests that these texts are most likely to be forgeries, which their authors attributed to their early Pythagorean predecessors to gain philosophical weight. The corpus includes ten letters – eight of which are ascribed to Theano, one to Myia, and one to an author named Melissa – and at least five treatises – *On Piety*, which is also ascribed to Theano; *On Wisdom* and *On the Harmony of Women* by Perictione; *On the Moderation of Women* by Phintys; and *On Human Nature* by Aesara. As a result, there is evidence of women partaking in both stages of Pythagoreanism: its emergence and first development in the 5th century

---

[8] On Neopythagoreanism in Rome and Asia Minor, see Flinterman (2014). On the Neopythagorean Platonists, see Dillon (2014). Zhmud distinguishes a third group of Pythagorean mystics who lived between the late 4th century BCE and the 1st century BCE, such as Diodorus of Aspendus and Androcydes, whom he labels as 'post-Pythagoreans' (2012b: 228–30). For a threefold periodisation of the Pythagorean tradition, see also Haskins (2005: 315).

and its Hellenistic and post-Hellenistic renaissance. In the first phase, women take part in Pythagorean societies but leave no writings. In the second phase, numerous texts survive, but the identity of their authors, especially those writings under female names, is debated.

1.1.1 Source Problems

The source issue is most effectively summarised by Barbara Graziosi in her review of Sarah Pomeroy's monograph on the Pythagorean women: 'There is little evidence about either Pythagoras or women in antiquity, let alone a combination of the two' (2013).

The surviving evidence for early Pythagorean societies and thinkers is scant and controversial. The challenges are threefold: the lack of direct evidence, the status of the surviving indirect sources, and the presence of forgeries. First, up until the time of Philolaus in the late 5th century and then Archytas in the 4th century, the Pythagoreans left no written works and kept most of their doctrines secret.[9] Second, the indirect evidence available to us is meagre, highly debated, predominantly post-Platonic, and often conflicting over significant points. The most reliable sources are the Peripatetic biographers Aristoxenus of Tarentum and Dicaearchus of Messana in the 4th century BCE and 3rd-century historians such as Timaeus of Tauromenium and Neanthes of Cyzicus. Aristoxenus' account is especially valuable, for he was originally from Tarentum, where the Pythagorean Archytas lived;[10] then moved to Phlius, which hosted a large Pythagorean community (Iamb. *VP* 267); and finally studied in Athens under Xenophilus, a pupil of Philolaus, known as one of 'the last Pythagoreans' (D.L. 8.46). Similarly, another helpful intermediary source is Timaeus, who wrote a history of Magna Graecia and thus had substantial data about early Pythagoreanism in Southern Italy. Nevertheless, these accounts were written centuries after

---

[9] See Isocrates, *Busiris* 29; Aristoxenus, Fr. 43; D.L. 8.15; Porph. *VP* 57; Iamb. *VP* 163, 199, 226–7, 246–7. Some members might even have been expelled for publishing the secrets. See, for example, Empedocles in D.L. 8.54, on the evidence of Timaeus and Hippasus in Iamb. *VP* 75, 246. On the possibility that some doctrines, such as the transmigration of souls, escaped the vow of silence, see Porph. *VP* 19. In the 3rd century, both Diogenes and Iamblichus refer to some, arguably apocryphal, writings by Pythagoras: the treatises mentioned by Heraclitus (D.L. 8.6–7 – see DK 22 B129), a letter to Anaximenes (D.L. 8.49), his memoirs (D.L. 8.42; Iamb. *VP* 146 – see Laks, 2014: 371–7), and a book titled *Sacred Discourse* (Iamb. *VP* 259 – see Thesleff, 1965: 158.8–168.12). On the existence of spurious Pythagorean texts, see Iamb. *VP* 2. For a discussion of Pythagorean secrecy, see Burkert (1972: 178–9). *Contra* Zhmud, according to whom the Pythagoreans are simply restrained in speech (2012a: 150–65). Regardless of whether Pythagoras left writings of any sort, no direct evidence of pre-Philolaic Pythagoreanism was preserved.

[10] Archytas was an acquaintance of Sphintarus, the father of Aristoxenus (Frs. 1, 19, 20, 30). On Aristoxenus, see Huffman (2012).

Pythagoras' death and are now partially lost. By contrast, the most extensive sources available to us are the three *Lives* of Pythagoras by Diogenes Laertius, Porphyry, and Iamblichus written in the 3rd century CE, whose reliability is nonetheless highly debated by scholars.[11]

Finally, as previously mentioned, in antiquity, there was a tendency to forge Pythagorean writings and attribute later, especially Platonic, philosophical positions back to Pythagoras. The outcome is that the available apocryphal texts outnumber the evidence about original Pythagoreanism. In what follows, I shall begin by reviewing the evidence from those 4th-century sources that are closer to the early Pythagoreans and less likely to have been influenced by the Platonic tradition. Next, I move on to the pseudepigrapha as a different, but not less valuable, manifestation of Pythagoreanism.

Though fragmentary and disputed, these sources consistently refer to Pythagoras' female followers. Specifically, the textual evidence for the Pythagorean women can be organised into three groups: the fragments *about* women, the sayings allegedly *by* women, and the writings *ascribed to* Pythagorean female pseudepigraphers. We first find brief references to women following Pythagoras in the 4th- and 3rd-century accounts of early Pythagoreanism.[12] These passages are later quoted in the *Lives* by Diogenes, Porphyry, and Iamblichus, together with lengthier and unevidenced anecdotes regarding Pythagoras' teachings to his female pupils. I shall analyse this evidence in Section 2. The second group comprises the maxims and moral precepts ascribed to Theano, Pythagoras' wife.[13] Finally, in the 5th century CE, the anthologist Stobaeus compiles a collection of extracts from earlier Greek authors, titled *Eclogues*, which includes the Pythagorean women's pseudepigrapha.[14] I turn to these texts in Section 3.[15]

---

[11] On the *Lives*, see Laks (2014); Macris (2014); O'Meara (2014). On Aristoxenus and Dicaearchus, see Fortenbaugh (2007); Huffman (2014b: 274–96, 2019). On Pythagoras in the historical tradition, see Schorn (2014). On source problems in general, see Burkert (1972: 97–109); Dillon and Hershbell (1991: 4–14); Zhmud (2012a: 8–15, 25–77); Huffman (2018).

[12] I include in this group the fragments by the 4th-century comic poets Alexis and Cratinus the Younger, both of whom wrote plays titled *Pythagorizousa* (*The Female Disciple of Pythagoras*), cited by Athenaeus (4.161c–d) and Diogenes (8.37). See Dutsch (2020: 86–9).

[13] See, for example, the saying against adultery in D.L. 8.43, which is discussed in Section 2.2.3. For the purpose of this Element, I will not analyse the sayings in detail. For a thorough study of this evidence and other maxims reported by Plutarch, Clement of Alexandria, and Stobaeus, see Montepaone (2011: 32–6); Dutsch (2020: 71–114).

[14] I add to this group a fragment from a text on the immortality of the soul attributed to Theano in Clement's 2nd-century collection *Stromata* (4.7.44.2).

[15] The Pythagorean women's texts were translated into German in Wieland's 'Die Pythagorischen Frauen' (1789), into French in Meunier's *Femmes Pythagoriciennes* (1932), into Italian in Montepaone's *Pitagoriche* (2011), and recently into English by Plant (2004), Harper (in Pomeroy, 2013), and Dutsch (2020). For the original Greek, I refer to the collection of

1.2 The *Status Quaestionis* from Ménage to Dutsch

Modern scholars' engagement with the Pythagorean women started in 1690 in France with the publication of Gilles Ménage's *Historia Mulierum Philosopharum*. Ménage was profoundly interested in ancient Greek authors: after publishing a detailed commentary of Diogenes Laertius' *The Lives of Eminent Philosophers* in 1663, he decided to compile his own philosophical history, this time focusing on women philosophers. This is meant both as a supplement to Diogenes' work and as Ménage's own contribution to the *querelle des femmes* and the early feminist debates in the 17th century. The purpose is to challenge the assumption that there had been no women philosophers up to the early modern period and collect the available, though slim, information about women who devoted themselves to philosophy in Greek and Roman antiquity. The result is a list of sixty-five names, organised by schools, starting from women Platonists and closing with the Pythagoreans, who are introduced as the best-documented case of female participation in an ancient philosophical community. The chapter notoriously opens as follows: 'It could seem remarkable that there were so many Pythagorean women philosophers when the Pythagoreans had to observe silence for five years and had many secrets which they were not allowed to divulge, as women are very talkative and can scarcely keep a secret' (1984: 47, trans. Zedler).

The 20th century has seen a revival of academic interest in the Pythagorean women. Specifically, there are two trends: scholars working to reclaim women's place in the history of philosophy have devoted substantial space to the Pythagorean women, whereas scholars of Pythagoreanism acknowledge the unusual role women played in the Pythagorean tradition in more general terms.

Historians of women philosophers can be divided further into three groups. The initial tendency has been to trust the evidence for women in Pythagoreanism despite the many source issues. Mary Ellen Waithe and Kathleen Wider start from the premise that 'there were women involved with philosophy throughout ancient Greek history' (Wider, 1986: 22)[16] and that Pythagoras is the earliest and best-known philosopher to admit women among his disciples. They then analyse the available information and extant writings as historically accurate data and draw two conclusions: first of all, the letters and treatises were written by women philosophers, and second, some of them can be

---

Pythagorean writings by Thesleff (1965). The letters have also been edited by Hercher (1873) and Städele (1980).

[16] See also Waithe (1987: 5–9). Another scholar adopting inclusive criteria for ancient women philosophers is Warren (2009: 4). By contrast, Snyder (1991) and Plant (2004) focus exclusively on those women who left written works, which still includes the authors of the Pythagorean pseudepigrapha.

dated as early as the 5th century BCE. Similarly, more recently, Sarah Pomeroy has argued that the female point of view in the Pythagorean pseudepigrapha shows that they were in fact written by women (2013: xv–xxii). These studies have been an invaluable first step for the scholarship on the Pythagorean women.

Scholars have since then reacted to such charitable and optimistic interpretations of the evidence. Two examples of this more sceptic and cautious approach are Claudia Montepaone, who acknowledges the difficulty of retrieving reliable information about Theano and assessing the philosophical value of her teachings (1993: 75–105), and Marguerite Deslauriers, who calls attention to the challenges of studying the Pythagorean women, with special focus on the fragmentary nature of the evidence and the possibility that the Pythagorean pseudepigrapha might have in fact been written by men under female pseudonyms to address an audience of women (2012: 343–9).[17]

Finally, in the ongoing attempt to do justice to women philosophers from the past but with renewed attention to the source issues, the scholarship has started to deviate from the question of the historicity of the Pythagorean women and examine their reception instead. Since the Pythagorean apocrypha are written under pseudonyms, they can give us very limited information about the original authors. Thus, rather than discussing who these women were, when they lived, and who the real authors behind the pseudepigrapha might be, scholars now focus on the content of the texts and what they can tell us about the role of the Pythagorean women in ancient Greek culture: for example, Annette Huizenga has studied the pseudepigrapha in the context of Greek rhetoric in late antiquity (2013), and recently, Dorota Dutsch has contextualised these texts within the ancient Greek literary and philosophical tradition (2020).[18]

That of the Pythagorean women, then, is an emerging study, which so far has been primarily pursued by scholars of women philosophers. In addition, more emphasis has been placed on the Pythagorean women's writings of the Hellenistic period. By contrast, because of the scarcity of sources, the early Pythagorean women and the female status in 5th-century Pythagorean societies have received far less attention in the academic discourse, featuring mostly as brief references in the works of scholars of Pythagoreanism. De Vogel analyses Pythagoras' public speeches, which include his teachings on

---

[17] For a cautious, but nonetheless detailed, review of the evidence for ancient Greek female philosophers, see also Hawley (1994). The authorship of the pseudepigrapha is discussed further in Section 3.1.2.

[18] For an earlier study of the Pythagorean women as philosophers, see Nails (1989).

the husband–wife relationship (1966: 110–52), and briefly alludes to the actual presence of women in the communities (238, n. 2). Burkert notes that women were part of Pythagoras' cohort of disciples (1972: 122)[19] and cites Theano as Pythagoras' wife and the most famous Pythagorean woman (114) but discards the mathematical treatise *On Piety*, which is ascribed to Theano, as 'curious'. Zhmud lists the names of the women from Pythagoras' family (2012a: 103) but classifies the rest of the Pythagorean women as literary characters (180). Finally, Huffman acknowledges that women 'may have indeed played an *unusually large* role in Pythagoreanism' (Huffman, 2019, emphasis added) and gives a brief account of Theano's life.[20] Two exceptions worth mentioning are Constantinos Macris' detailed entries on the Pythagorean women in the *Dictionnaire des philosophes antiques* (2016) and Catherine Rowett's reconstruction of women's role in early Pythagorean politics (2014: 122–3).[21]

Overall, there is almost unanimous consensus among scholars that the Pythagorean women and their pseudepigrapha deserve more and more thorough attention. The question is how to approach them. This Element builds on Dorota Dutsch's work on the Pythagorean women by highlighting their contributions to the ancient Pythagorean tradition and more generally Greek philosophy, from the 5th century BCE to the pseudepigrapha. Rather than viewing the Pythagorean women as historical figures, I am interested in considering them as philosophers.

2 Early Pythagoreanism: Not Only for Men, But Also for Women

This Element revolves around the question 'What kind of philosopher is the Pythagorean woman?' I answer this question by looking at both the evidence for women in early Pythagorean societies and the Pythagorean pseudepigrapha ascribed to female authors. In the case of early Pythagoreanism, our main question should be unpacked into two issues: (1) what counts as philosophy for Pythagoras and his early followers? And (2) how did the early Pythagorean women contribute to this project?

---

[19] See also Burkert (1982: 17–18); Kingsley (1995: 149–72).

[20] See Huffman (2018): 'Women were probably more active in Pythagoreanism than in any other philosophical movement. ... Pythagoreanism is the philosophical school that gave most prominence to women'. See also Cornelli (2013: 57–8, 74–5): 'Among the practices that mark off the Pythagorean community from the rest of Greek society is the admission of women to the same social status of men'; Centrone (2014: 45): 'Whatever may have been the nature of the ancient Pythagorean fellowship, it seems clear that women played a prominent role in it'; and Riedweg (2015: 96): 'Women seem to have played in Pythagoreanism a role unparalleled in other philosophical movements'.

[21] Another scholar of ancient philosophy discussing the early Pythagorean women is Demand (1982: 132–5). See also Pellò (2020b).

2.1 The Pythagorean Way of Life

There are several unsolved puzzles surrounding the 5th-century Pythagorean communities. One such issue, possibly the most challenging one, is what sort of doctrines Pythagoras taught his disciples (Lloyd, 2014). Far from solving the puzzle, I shall simply draw attention to Plato's own answer.

There are at least three theories our sources describe as central to ancient Pythagoreanism: the belief in the reincarnation of souls, some kind of number doctrine, and the way of life.[22] The earliest surviving evidence pictures Pythagoras as an authority on the afterlife and metempsychosis. For example, one of Pythagoras' contemporaries, the philosopher Xenophanes, ridicules him for recognising the soul of an old friend in a barking dog (DK 21 B7, in D.L. 8.36).[23] On the other hand, in the *Metaphysics*, Aristotle describes the Pythagoreans as those who 'devote themselves to mathematics' and believe that numbers are the principles of all things (1.5.985b23–24).[24] Plato, in turn, characterises early Pythagoreanism as follows:

> If not in public, was Homer considered a guide in private education, when he was alive, for those who enjoyed his company, and handed down to posterity some kind of Homeric way of living, as Pythagoras himself was especially honoured for this and to this day his followers are somehow distinguished from others by calling their way of life Pythagorean? (Pl. *Rep.* 10.600a–b)

Pythagoras taught his disciples a peculiar way of life, and the Pythagoreans distinguished themselves from others by living in accordance with Pythagoras' teachings. Specifically, Pythagoras is known for regulating his followers' *private* lives. According to Plato, then, the lifestyle is the essence and hallmark of ancient Pythagoreanism. It is the distinctive trait identifying someone as a Pythagorean and separating him, or her, from the non-Pythagoreans more than any number or soul theories.[25]

---

[22] For a discussion of the criteria for ancient Pythagoreanism, see Huffman (2008b: 292–302); Zhmud (2012a: 119–34). Zhmud criticises the doctrinal criterion, according to which all Pythagoreans believe in the afterlife or study mathematics, and proposes a family resemblance criterion, according to which among the Pythagoreans there is not one single shared feature, but rather a series of overlapping similarities.

[23] Other early sources for Pythagorean metempsychosis are Herodotus (2.81, 2.123, 4.95), Ion (D. L. 1.120), and Empedocles (DK 31 B129, quoted in Timaeus (*FGrHist* 566 Fr. 14); D.L. 8.54; Porph. *VP* 30; Iamb. *VP* 67). See Pellò (2018).

[24] It should be noted that Aristotle links mathematics with a group of 5th-century philosophers he describes as so-called Pythagoreans. For a detailed analysis of this report, see Primavesi (2014). On mathematics as central to mainstream Pythagoreanism, see Schofield (2012: 142).

[25] Pythagoras' opponents, too, criticised his followers for their unusual way of living (Dichaearchus Fr. 34 (Wehrli, 1974); Porph. *VP* 56; Iamb. *VP* 255). On the way of life as the distinctive trait of Pythagoreanism, see Huffman (2008b: 292–301); Cornelli (2013: 55–62);

According to our sources, Pythagoras would educate his audiences and regulate their way of living in at least two steps: public lectures and secret teachings.[26] As detailed in Section 2.2.1, Pythagoras' career as an educator begins at his arrival in Southern Italy.[27] Once in Croton, Pythagoras is said to have delivered four public lectures: to the magistrates in the council chamber (Iamb. *VP* 45), to the youths in the gymnasium (37), to the boys in the temple of Apollo (50), and to the women in the temple of Hera (56).[28] Among these audiences, some followers are then admitted into Pythagoras' intellectual circles.[29] The selected disciples are educated via short sayings, precepts, and maxims, which are delivered orally and mostly kept secret. The prescriptions take the name of *akousmata* ('things heard') or *symbola* ('passwords').[30] Thus, the available evidence for the Pythagorean way of life is twofold: the Crotonian speeches[31] and the *akousmata*.[32] The former includes generally sound advice on

---

Macris (2013). *Contra* Zhmud, according to whom the evidence is too limited to show what this lifestyle might comprise (2012a: 111).

[26] In the *Lives*, Pythagoras' disciples are divided into various subgroups, among which the best-known are the *akousmatici*, hearers, who simply abide by Pythagoras' life regulations, and the *mathematici*, mathematicians, who engage with his number doctrines (Porph. *VP* 37; Iamb. *VP* 29–30, 72–4, 80–2, 88–9). However, the evidence for this is late, conflicting, and of dubious reliability. For a discussion of the surviving reports, see Cornelli (2013: 77–83); Horky (2013: 3–35, 85–124). *Contra* Zhmud (2012a: 169–92).

[27] Porphyry writes that Pythagoras founded his first school, called Pythagorean Semicircles, before travelling to Italy (*VP* 9). According to Aristoxenus, Pythagoras left the island of Samos in Ionia under the tyranny of Polycrates (Fr. 16, in Porph. *VP* 9, 16; D.L. 8.3; Iamb. *VP* 11). Aristoxenus writes that Pythagoras was forty when Polycrates came to power (540/535 BCE, according to Hdt. 3.39), which would date his birth around 590 BCE and his exile from Samos in 530 BCE. Rowett suggests a different chronology and dates Pythagoras' arrival in Croton in 510 BCE (2014: 112–3). On the ancient debate over Pythagoras' origins, see D.L. 8.1; Porph. *VP* 1–2. For a discussion of the evidence, see Philip (1966: 185–99); Burkert (1972: 110–20).

[28] See Antisthenes Fr. 51 (Caizzi, 1966); Dicaearchus Fr. 33, in Porph. *VP* 18–19. The evidence is quoted in full and discussed in Section 2.2.1.

[29] For a late and anecdotal description of the examination and initiation the Pythagoreans are allegedly required to undergo before entering the community, see D.L. 8.10; Iamb. *VP* 69–74.

[30] For a list of *akousmata*, see Chapter 18 of Iamblichus' *Vita* (82–6), which Burkert takes to be quoted from Aristotle (1972: 170). Further examples are found in D.L. 8.34–5 and Porph. *VP* 41–2. The *symbola* are listed in Aristoxenus Fr. 43; D.L. 8.15–7; Iamb. *VP* 103–5, 227, 238.

[31] A version of the speeches is reported in full by Iamblichus (*VP* 37–57). It is unlikely that these were quoted *verbatim* from Pythagoras. Rather, there were arguably composed sometime in the Hellenistic period on the evidence of earlier, but nonetheless post-Pythagorean, sources, such as Aristoxenus, Timaeus, and Apollonius (Rostagni, 1955–1956: 35–56; De Vogel, 1966: 140–7; Burkert, 1972: 100–15;). Nonetheless, unlike the pseudepigrapha, the speeches are relatively homogeneous and have no strong Platonic, Aristotelian, and Stoic undertones, which suggest that they did not result from layering of different philosophical traditions (Centrone, 1996; Macris, 2013: 71). This then leaves open the possibility that the speeches might be reconstructions of Pythagoras' original teachings to and about women and that some passages might hark back to 5th-century Pythagoreanism.

[32] On the *akousmata* as reliable evidence for the Pythagorean way of life, see Burkert (1972: 166–92); Kirk, Raven, and Schofield (1983: 229–30); Huffman (2008a: 105–6). *Contra* Zhmud (2012a: 192–205). The first collection of Pythagorean precepts was published in the 4th century

how to behave in one's everyday life. The latter are puzzling and demanding precepts on topics ranging from religious rituals and behavioural norms to eating habits and dietary vetoes, whose meaning and rationale are unknown to outsiders.[33] Together, these sources give a thumbnail sketch of what living like a Pythagorean might have entailed.

Overall, Plato's account in the *Republic* is relevant on two counts: first, it offers a preliminary solution to the question of how the early Pythagoreans would practise philosophy. What it means to be a philosopher in Greek antiquity before Plato and Aristotle is a vexed question.[34] According to Plato, in the case of the Pythagoreans, this might have something to do with living a philosophical way of life – that is, a life that conforms to Pythagoras' doctrines, teachings, and precepts.[35] Second, the focus on private life extends Pythagoras' teachings to the domestic sphere. If being a Pythagorean involved living like a Pythagorean from daybreak to nightfall, from birth to funeral rituals, in private as well as in public, being brought up according to Pythagorean doctrines and implementing them from the earliest stages in one's family life would be the first step towards becoming a true follower.[36] This links the early Pythagoreans and their way of life to the women.[37] Rowett argues that Pythagoras makes women 'part of an intellectual project' (2014: 122), for they have a role in perpetuating the Pythagorean lifestyle.[38] As I argue in the next section, they do so both as mothers and as teachers.

BCE by Anaximander the Younger (*Suda* 1987, s.v. Anaximandros), whose collection provides the foundations for Aristotle's works on the Pythagoreans (Frs. 195–6 (Rose 1886), in D.L. 8.34–5; Porph. *VP* 41), which are now unfortunately lost. Further evidence comes in the 1st century BCE from Androcydes (Iamb. *VP* 146) and the erudite scholar Alexander Polyhistor (D.L. 8.24–33).

[33] See, for example, 'Do not stir the fire with a knife!' in Porph. *VP* 42. For a detailed discussion, see Vítek (2009: 247–53).

[34] Pythagoras was believed to have invented the word *philosophos*, lover of wisdom (D.L. 1.12), which at the time was not an established profession nor a set discipline. For a discussion of the historical accuracy of this anecdote, see Riedweg (2005: 90–7). *Contra* Burkert (1960); Zhmud (2012a: 428–30).

[35] The best-known account of ancient Greek philosophy as a way of life is Hadot (1995, 2002). For a connection between this view and Pythagoreanism, see Macris (2013).

[36] In the *Vita Pythagorica*, arguably on the evidence of Aristoxenus (Dillon and Hershbell, 1991: 121), Iamblichus describes the average Pythagorean day, including morning walks and exercises, midday intellectual exchanges, common meals, evening libations, and the prohibition on wearing wool (96–100). This shows that Pythagoras' prescriptions regulated various aspects of his followers' lives, from politics to food consumption and dietary taboos, including aspects that were traditionally associated with the female gender, such as religious rituals. For a review of the evidence, see Gemelli Marciano (2014: 145–6).

[37] Interestingly, Aristoxenus suggests that Pythagoras learnt his 'ethical' doctrines from a woman, the priestess Themistoclea (Fr. 15). On Themistoclea (or Theoclea), see Section 2.2.2.

[38] On women being part of an ethical programme and all-embracing lifestyle, see also Pomeroy (2013: xix, 11–13).

2.2 The 'Most Famous' Pythagorean Women

The argument is that the Pythagorean women engage with the community alongside men by practising the Pythagorean way of life and carrying out Pythagoras' norms and precepts. This, in turn, raises a number of questions: did Pythagoras and the early Pythagoreans deliver lectures specifically for women, which would show that they were interested in educating them? If so, are these teachings exclusively centred on family life? Were women mere listeners, or did this philosophical lifestyle allow for further engagement with Pythagorean doctrines? For example, could women act as teachers?

Our sources paint three different pictures. (1) The Pythagorean women are first introduced as students of Pythagoras and attendees at his public lectures. A list of seventeen names collected by Iamblichus suggests that they are also members of his restricted intellectual circles. Yet, while Pythagoras' interest in educating women is described as unconventional, there is no evidence that these women are in turn viewed as intellectuals themselves. Moreover, the limited evidence of Pythagoras' teachings to and about women suggests that they are trained to be wives and mothers. Next, (2) from the 3rd century BCE, we find references to the women of Pythagoras' family. Again, however, the evidence does not go beyond domestic life, and the Pythagorean women are not attributed philosophical ideas of their own. Finally, (3) one fragment by Neanthes and a few precepts ascribed to Theano suggest that at least some women receive a similar education and practise the same philosophical way of life as the Pythagorean men and are viewed as intellectual authorities on both ethical and theoretical matters.

2.2.1 The Pythagorean Women as Students

The earliest evidence for female Pythagoreans focuses not on the women themselves but on Pythagoras and his skills as an educator.[39] Women are mentioned to the extent that they are Pythagoras' students and listen to his public lectures. The source is the 5th-century orator and philosopher Antisthenes, a pupil of Socrates. The fragment is about Odysseus: Antisthenes explains the meaning of the Greek adjective *polytropos* (versatile or multifaceted) by comparing Odysseus to Pythagoras in virtue of their ability to interact with different people in different and fitting ways.

> Thus, people say that Pythagoras too, deemed worthy to lecture the children, composed playful speeches for them, and to the women he delivered speeches

---

[39] Dutsch describes these as 'glimpses of Pythagorean women from a distance' (2020: 15).

that are suitable for women, and to the magistrates speeches suitable for
rulers, and to the youths speeches suitable for adolescence. For finding
a method of learning that fits each audience is a sign of wisdom, whereas it
is a sign of ignorance to use one kind of speech for different audiences.

(Antisthenes Fr. 51, Scholia to *Odyssey* 1.1)

According to Antisthenes' report, Pythagoras was famous for tailoring his
lectures to the audience: youthful speeches for the youths, leader-like speeches
for the rulers, childlike speeches for children, and feminine speeches for
women. Different groups of pupils are educated differently, depending on
their age, gender, and social role. As an orator himself, Antisthenes takes this
to be a sign of wisdom. The first mention of the Pythagorean women, then, is as
witnesses to Pythagoras' own mastery.

From the fragment, we can draw two consequences: first, Pythagoras was
committed to educating all sorts of disciples, including women. Second, women
have separate and different educational experiences from men. A similar point
is made a century later by Dicaearchus, a student of Aristotle. Dicaearchus is
a biographer and one of our most reliable sources for early Pythagorean societies. In this fragment, he describes Pythagoras' arrival in Southern Italy and the
beginning of his philosophical career.

When he came to Italy and stopped at Croton, Dicaearchus says, he arrived
as a great traveller, gifted by his own nature, and prosperously guided by
fortune. He gave the Crotoniates the impression of a free and great man,
graceful and elegant in speech, gesture, and all other things, so that he
inspired the council of elders by discussing many fine things with them.
They appointed him to give youthful lectures to the youths, and then to the
boys who came from school to hear him; and then to the women – even
a meeting of women was arranged for him. Through this, his great reputation grew further, he drew great audiences from the city – not only men, but
also women, among whom was Theano – and many also from the neigh-
bouring foreign regions, kings, and rulers.

(Dicaearchus Fr. 33/40, in Porph. *VP* 18–19)

Pythagoras is again portrayed as an exceptional teacher. The reason is twofold:
the content and the style of his lectures. First, Pythagoras teaches 'many fine
things' to his pupils. Second, he is able to address and educate a wide variety of
audiences. Each time, the speeches are appropriate to the listeners: for example,
he gives 'youthful' lectures to the young. Dicaearchus mentions the same
groups Antisthenes lists: first, Pythagoras teaches the magistrates, who then
ask him to lecture the Crotonian youths and children. Finally, and most importantly, for the purpose of this Element, they arrange for him to deliver a lecture to
the women. That Dicaearchus is calling attention to the latter speech is

evidenced by two features: first, the emphatic way in which Dicaearchus introduces the gathering of women ('*even* a meeting of women was arranged for him').[40] Second, as a result of the successful Crotonian speeches, Pythagoras is said to attract even greater audiences, which include 'not only men, *but also* women'. When quoting Dicaearchus' fragment, Porphyry supplements his testimony with a remark from the 2nd-century Neopythagorean philosopher Nicomachus, according to whom the speeches were so persuasive that Pythagoras gained more than two thousand followers and they built 'a large auditorium together with women and children' (Porph. *VP* 20).[41] This suggests that, unlike lecturing the boys and the youths, educating the female gender in public was unconventional and unheard-of. One woman, Theano, is even singled out and mentioned by name.[42]

The reports by Antisthenes and Dicaearchus refer to the first stage of Pythagorean education: the public lectures to the people of Croton. The claim is that the inclusion of women is somewhat exceptional and, as such, is a sign of Pythagoras' skills as a teacher and a public speaker. However, the evidence also shows that the Crotonian men and women are kept separate, attend Pythagoras' lectures in different groups, and do not share learning. Moreover, these two fragments only picture Pythagoras delivering public speeches to men and women without clarifying whether female pupils are also admitted to his selective groups of disciples. When quoting from Dicaearchus, Porphyry distinguishes the open lectures Pythagoras gives to the Crotoniates regardless of age, gender, and status from the teachings he reserves for his followers, whose content is kept secret ('What he told his companions, one cannot say for certain, for the silence among his followers was not accidental', *VP* 19). While the speeches are public, what Pythagoras tells his companions is unknown. The question is whether the latter restricted group also includes women.

The first reference to women who are called Pythagoreans not only insofar as they listen to Pythagoras' speeches[43] but also as they join his circles of followers

---

[40] See also Rowett (2014: 114–5).

[41] The same account is quoted almost *verbatim* by Iamblichus (*VP* 29–30).

[42] The one quoted above (by Dicaearchus) is Mirhady's edition in Fortenbaugh and Schütrumpf (2018: Ch. 1, Fr. 40). In Wehrli's edition of the same fragment (Fr. 33), the last sentence is taken to be an interpolation by Porphyry, who adds the example of Theano as the best-known Pythagorean woman. However, earlier in the *Life* Porphyry introduces Theano as Pythagoras' wife (4), whereas in this passage she is said to be simply one of Pythagoras' pupils. The inconsistency suggests that the source of the example is Dicaearchus himself rather than Porphyry. This in turn shows that Theano's engagement with Pythagoreanism is attested as early as the 4th century BCE.

[43] On the evidence of Hermippus, a 3rd-century Peripatetic philosopher, Diogenes writes that the women who had attended Pythagoras' lectures are called *pythagorikas*, Pythagorean (Fr. 20, in D.L. 8.41).

is the so-called *Catalogue of the Pythagoreans*. The *Catalogue* consists of a list of 235 names of Pythagorean followers, attached to the final chapter of Iamblichus' *Vita Pythagorica*, which describes the community after Pythagoras' death. It comprises the names of 218 Pythagorean men, organised into 28 groups based on their city of origin, and 17 women. The list is not meant to be exhaustive. Iamblichus writes that Pythagoras had many more followers whose names are unknown to him. Similarly, the women are introduced as the 'most famous' among Pythagoras' female disciples, which suggests that there were more.

> The most famous Pythagorean women are: Timycha, wife of Myllias of Croton; Philtys, daughter of Theophris of Croton and sister of Byndacos; Occelo and Eccelo, sisters of the Lucanians Occelus and Occilus; Cheilonis, daughter of Cheilon the Lacedaimonian; Cratesicleia the Laconian, wife of Cleanor the Lacedaemonian; Theano, wife of Brotinus of Metapontum; Myia, wife of Milon of Croton; Lastheneia from Arcadia;[44] Habroteleia, daughter of Habroteles of Tarentum; Echecrateia of Phlius; Tyrsenis from Sybaris; Peisirrhode from Tarentum; Theadusa the Laconian; Boeo from Argos; Babelyca from Argos; Cleaichma, sister of Autocharidas the Lacedaemonian. In total, they are seventeen. (Iamb. *VP* 267)

Unlike the men, only seven women are listed with their city of origin: Lastheneia, Echecrateia, Tyrsenis, Peisirrhode, Theadusa, Boeo, and Babelyca. The other ten women are listed alongside the names of their fathers, husbands, and brothers, some of whom, like Myllias and Milon, are listed among the Pythagorean men in the first part of the *Catalogue*. As I discuss in Sections 2.2.2 and 2.2.3, Timycha, Theano, and Myia are also mentioned in other sources on ancient Pythagoreanism, including Dicaearchus and Neanthes. Other women, such as Habroteleia and Occelo, seem to be named after their better-known fathers and brothers.[45] Finally, some names are not attested in any other ancient source.[46] This makes the *Catalogue* a valuable piece of evidence

---

[44] Diogenes identifies Lastheneia as one of the few female disciples of Plato (3.46, on the evidence of Dicaearchus Fr. 44) and Sepusippus (4.2). He suggests that she was able to join the Academy by disguising herself as a man. See Dorandi (1989); Reeve (2000).

[45] Occelo's brother Occelus is the named author of two pseudepigraphic treatises titled *On Law* (Stob. 1.13.2; Thesleff, 1965: 124.16–125.7) and *On the Nature of the Universe* (Stob. 1.20.3–5; Thesleff, 1965: 125.9–138.22). For another mention of Occelus among the early Pythagoreans, see Cens. 4.3. Stobaeus also quotes a treatise titled *On Justice* and attributed it to 'the Lucanian Pythagorean man (*pythagoreiou*) Eccelus' (3.9.51; Thesleff 77.16). Therefore, whilst in the *Catalogue* Eccelo is listed among the Pythagorean women, the treatise by Eccelus is not included among the writings ascribed to Pythagorean female authors. The reason for the confusion might be that since the names of the four Lucanian siblings are similar, they could get mixed up with one another. It should be noted that the female author Aesara is also introduced as a Pythagorean man (*pythagoreiou*, see Section 3.2.1).

[46] For a detailed prosopography of the Pythagorean women, see Pomeroy (2013: 1–7).

in support of the claim that not only did Pythagoras lecture women at his arrival in Croton, but he also welcomed some of them among his followers.

The difficulties of relying on the *Catalogue* are twofold: first, Iamblichus is a late and partially unreliable source, and second, this list does not give any clues as to the intellectual contributions of the women. Iamblichus writes in the 3rd century CE when the Pythagorean women's pseudepigrapha are already in circulation. These texts contribute to the belief that women are part of Pythagorean societies and may have influenced Iamblichus' decision to add the *Catalogue of the Pythagorean Women* at the end of the *Vita*. Moreover, many of the female names are not attested in any other source of evidence for early Pythagoreanism, which raises doubts over their historicity. The solution to this first issue lies in the dating of the *Catalogue*. There is consensus among scholars in attributing the *Catalogue* to Aristoxenus in the 4th century BCE.[47] The reasons for this are threefold. First, Iamblichus is unlikely to be the original compiler. Second, the *Catalogue* seems to have been assembled in the 4th century BCE. Third, among the 4th-century authors, Aristoxenus is the most promising candidate.

The argument against attributing the *Catalogue* to Iamblichus is that the list includes 145 names that are not mentioned anywhere else in his *Vita Pythagorica*. As such, the *Catalogue* appears as an isolated piece of evidence Iamblichus appends to his work. On the other hand, the *Catalogue* does not include the names of 18 Pythagoreans mentioned earlier in the *Vita*, including the physician Democedes (254, 261), who, according to Herodotus, was Pythagoras' grandson-in-law (3.137), and women such as Pythagoras' daughter Damo and granddaughter Bitale (146). Similarly, even though Theano features in three chapters of the *Vita*, Iamblichus usually identifies her as the wife of Pythagoras (146, 265) rather than of Brotinus. He even explicitly distinguishes her from the wife of Brotinus, whom he names Deino (132). According to Huffman, this simply shows that Iamblichus is not a methodical compiler (2008b: 298). Yet, since the *Catalogue* is introduced as the list of Pythagoreans 'whose names are known', the discrepancy between the Pythagoreans named earlier in Iamblichus' *Vita* and those considered most illustrious in the *Catalogue* suggests that he is more likely to have transferred the list from another source. The second reason for questioning Iamblichus' authorship and, alternatively, dating the *Catalogue* in the 4th century is that most names refer to first- and second-generation Pythagoreans. Specifically, there is no trace of the authors of the pseudepigrapha of Iamblichus' time.

---

[47] See Burkert (1972: 105, n. 40), Zhmud (2012a: 109–34; 2012b: 235–43). Yet the *Catalogue* is not included in Wehrli's collection of Aristoxenus' fragments.

Finally, the reason for ascribing the *Catalogue* specifically to Aristoxenus is that it includes information to which only a source as familiar with Pythagoreanism as Aristoxenus was would have had access. As Zhmud notices, the largest group in the *Catalogue* are the forty-five Pythagorean men and women from Tarentum, which is the birthplace of Aristoxenus (2012a: 112). Moreover, and most importantly, the cities of origin of some of the Pythagoreans in the *Catalogue* coincide with those mentioned in Aristoxenus' fragments: for example, Philolaus is traditionally identified as a Crotonian (D.L. 8.84), and yet both the *Catalogue* and Aristoxenus' Fr. 19 refer to Philolaus as a Pythagorean from Tarentum. Overall, although the *Catalogue* may well have undergone reworking, modifications, and interpolations, arguably even at the hands of Iamblichus himself, the 4th-century Peripatetic biographer Aristoxenus could be the ultimate source. Given Aristoxenus' acquaintance with Pythagorean societies, the *Catalogue*, and specifically the suggestion that some women are well-known members of Pythagoras' following, could then be relied upon.

One might finally object that the arguments for attributing the *Catalogue* to Aristoxenus are mostly based on the list of Pythagorean men, which leaves open the possibility that the female names were added at a later stage by a less reliable source. However, it is worth stressing that this is not the only early piece of evidence mentioning the Pythagorean women by name. For example, Timycha also features in a fragment by Neanthes (see Section 2.2.3). Another 4th-century name may be Echecrateia, which is likely to be connected to the Pythagorean Echecrates of Phlius from Plato's *Phaedo* (57a-58e). Thus, although it is possible that some names were added after the 4th century, the *Catalogue of the Pythagorean Women* still retains a layer of antiquity.[48]

The second, and more challenging, problem with the *Catalogue* is that it is unclear which criterion the original compiler might have used to determine who counts as a Pythagorean and who is to be left out. Most importantly, we do not know whether inclusion in the *Catalogue* should be taken as evidence of intellectual activity of any kind and, in the case of these seventeen women, as evidence of the same sort of intellectual activities as the other 218 men. Specifically, two pieces of evidence point to the contrary: first, as Antisthenes notes, Pythagoras is known for diversifying his teachings, distinguishing various groups of followers, and compartmentalising their knowledge. Second,

---

[48] An alternative source for the list of Pythagorean women could be the 3rd-century historian Philochorus, who lives soon after Aristoxenus and authors a book titled *The Assembly of Heroines or Pythagorean Women*, which is now unfortunately lost (Demand, 1982: 133). This would explain the inconsistencies between Aristoxenus' *Catalogue*, where the Pythagorean men are listed by city of origin, and the seventeen female disciples identified by family relations.

unlike the Pythagorean men, who are grouped based on where they are from, most women in the *Catalogue* are simply listed as mothers, sisters, wives, and daughters of other Pythagoreans. The doubt is that women could have been admitted into the societies together with their male relatives and in virtue of their traditional family roles.[49]

Further evidence for this comes from the surviving reconstructions of Pythagoras' teachings to women. In the previous section, I wrote that the Pythagorean women receive a two-stage education: the open lectures and the secret teachings for select groups of male and female disciples. As I noted, both sources of evidence are of doubtful reliability. My claim here is simply that, even if one were to take the speeches and the precepts as sources of evidence for early Pythagoreanism, they would nonetheless still picture the Pythagorean women as wives and mothers. In the *Vita Pythagorica*, Iamblichus records the content of four speeches by Pythagoras to the Crotonian magistrates, the boys, the youths, and the women (*VP* 37–57). The speech to the women includes advice about religion and family life. First, they are told to worship the gods with handmade nonanimal offerings, without the help of slaves, and without incurring great expenses (54). Second, they are urged to love their husbands more than they love their fathers, discouraged from disagreeing with either of them, allowed to make sacrifices after lying with their spouse, and forbidden from entering the temples after committing adultery (54–55). Third, women are encouraged to share their belongings with other women (55).[50] Finally, they are reminded to be pious and follow Odysseus' example by being faithful to their spouses (57). Therefore, women are primarily educated insofar as they are wives and household mistresses. The women who are then admitted into the community are taught via short sayings, called *akousmata*. Pythagoras is said to have formulated the following precepts: 'Do not beget children with a gold-wearing woman' and 'Do not drive your wife away, for she is a suppliant, for what reason we both lead her from the hearth and take her by the right hand' (Iamb. *VP* 84). Both precepts are about marital relationships. The former discourages Pythagoras' disciples from begetting children with courtesans,

---

[49] On the importance of family relations for female philosophers in antiquity, see Hawley (1994).

[50] The reference to the prohibition on killing animals and the instruction to hold property in common sound especially Pythagorean. Pythagoras was known for forbidding his disciples from killing, eating, and sacrificing animals. The reason behind this prohibition is debated and ranges from the belief in reincarnation of human souls into animal bodies (D.L. 8.13; Iamb. *VP* 85, 108, 168–9) to the need for a healthy diet and temperate lifestyle (Iamb. *VP* 187–213). Similarly, the Pythagoreans are known for living in a quasi-communist society and sharing their belongings. According to the historian Timaeus, Pythagoras is the author of the proverb 'common are the things of friends' (*koina ta philōn*, Fr. 13b – see D.L. 8.10; Porph. *VP* 33; Iamb. *VP* 92). This suggests that, besides being taught about their marital and religious duties, the Crotonian women might also be initiated into a specifically Pythagorean way of life.

whom Iamblichus distinguishes from married women in that they wear golden jewellery (*VP* 187).[51] The latter describes a marriage ritual, in which the groom leads his bride-to-be out of her father's house and pledges to protect her as a suppliant in need of asylum. Once again, the focus is on women's domestic role.[52]

Overall, Iamblichus' *Catalogue* is relevant for two reasons. First, this list confirms that Pythagoras' following includes both men and women. Second, it shows that not only are women part of Pythagoras' larger audiences but they are also admitted into his select group of disciples. Women are both the targets of Pythagoras' public lectures, as Antisthenes and Dicaearchus write, and members of his intellectual community of followers, as the *Catalogue* suggests. However, this still does not imply that they receive the same education as the men, nor does it allow any conclusions as to the content and philosophical value of their teachings. Women are part of the history of Pythagoreanism since the very beginning of Pythagoras' political and philosophical career in Croton. Yet our sources tend to distinguish them and their training from the men and restrict the latter to domesticity. This leads us to the next picture: the Pythagorean women as family members and, most importantly, the women of Pythagoras' own family.

2.2.2 The Pythagorean Women as Exemplary Wives and Daughters

Among the names from the *Catalogue* likely to hark back to the Classical Age, three women deserve special attention: Theano, Myia, and Timycha.

In the fragment by Dicaearchus quoted in the previous section, Theano is the only Pythagorean woman mentioned by name and singled out as the best-known of Pythagoras' female disciples. In Aristoxenus' *Catalogue*, she is one of the 'most famous' Pythagorean women and the wife of Brotinus of Metapontum. Later sources start to connect Theano to Pythagoras and portray her not only as a disciple but also as his wise spouse.[53] The earliest evidence for this is a fragment by the Hellenistic poet Hermesianax, quoted in Athenaeus' *Deipnosophistae*: 'Such was the love for Theano that bound up Pythagoras of

---

[51] Iamblichus adds that, after being lectured by Pythagoras, the Crotoniates dismissed their concubines (*VP* 132, 195). Pythagoras is also known for forbidding his disciples, particularly the women, from indulging in luxury. For example, in the Crotonian speeches women are advised against wearing expensive clothes. This suggests that the gold-wearing woman could be a non-Pythagorean woman.

[52] There is no evidence of *akousmata* for, rather than about, women. Yet our sources list some Hellenistic sayings ascribed to early Pythagorean women and addressed to their female disciples, which are analysed in Section 2.2.3.

[53] Alternatively, the only source listing Theano as Pythagoras' daughter is an anonymous *Life of Pythagoras*, copied in Photius' *Bibliotheca* in the 9th century CE (438b).

Samos' (Ath. 13.599a). Diogenes then distinguishes two traditions (8.42): some say that Theano was Brotinus' wife and Pythagoras' pupil, as exemplified in the *Catalogue*, whereas others consider Theano to be the daughter of Brotinus (who, in contrast with the *Catalogue*, is said to be from Croton) and the wife of Pythagoras.[54] Following the latter tradition, Porphyry introduces Theano as the daughter of Pythonax and the mother of Pythagoras' son Telauges and daughters Myia and Arignote (*VP* 4),[55] and Iamblichus writes that after Pythagoras' death his widow Theano married his successor Aristaeus (*VP* 255).[56] Diogenes also notes that, unlike her son Telauges, Theano is credited with producing written works (8.43). Whether this means that Theano broke the vow of silence and published her writings or rather, more likely, that in late antiquity, apocryphal treatises and collections of maxims were in circulation under Theano's name is an open question. Either way, Theano is primarily known as the wife of the wise Pythagoras and only secondarily as an intellectual herself.

The same can be said of Theano's daughter, Myia. The *Catalogue* lists Myia as Milon's wife. Quoting from Timaeus, Porphyry writes the following:

> Some write that from Theano, daughter of Pythonax from Crete, Pythagoras had a son Telauges and a daughter Myia, but others add Arignote. From them even Pythagorean texts have survived. Timaeus reports that, when she was still a girl, the daughter of Pythagoras was the first of the Crotonian maidens and then a wife among wives. He also writes that the people of Croton turned her house into a temple of Demeter and called the neighbouring street Museum. (Timaeus *FGrHist* 566 Fr. 131, in Porph. *VP* 4)

In the fragment, Timaeus praises Pythagoras' daughter, whom Porphyry later identifies as Myia. She is reputed to have outclassed the other Crotonian maidens to such extent that after her death, her house is turned into a temple of Demeter, and her street is dedicated to the Muses. Rowett takes the claim that Myia is superior to the women of Croton to suggest that she was an authoritative figure (2014: 123). Moreover, Porphyry allows for the

---

[54] The *Suda* also distinguishes two Theanos: one, referred to as Theano I, is the daughter of Leophron of Metapuntum and the wife of Brotinus of either Croton or Carystus (*Suda* 83, s.v. Theano); the other, referred to as Theano II, is from Crete and is the daughter of Pythonax, wife of Pythagoras, and mother to Telauges, Myia, Arignote, and Mnesarchus (84, s.v. Theano). The *Suda* entry on Pythagoras also lists Theano as his wife (3120, s.v. Pythagoras). On the distinction between two authors named Theano in the pseudepigrapha, see Section 3.1.1.

[55] Diogenes mentions another daughter named Damo and adds that Telauges was said to be Empedocles' teacher (DK 31 B155, in D.L. 8.42–3 – see also DK 31 A8, in Eus. *PE* 10.14.15). His source is an apocryphal letter from the Pythagorean Lysis to Hipparchus, which is discussed later. Telauges and Damo are also mentioned in Iamblichus' *Vita* (146).

[56] Two later sources, Eusebius (*PE* 10.14.14) and Theodoret (*Therapeutics* 2.23), report a slightly different anecdote, according to which Theano herself, together with her sons Telauges and Mnesachus, takes over the leadership of the community from Pythagoras. On Telauges succeeding his father, see also D.L. 8.8.

possibility that Pythagoras' daughters left written works.[57] Thus, regardless of whether the wise woman from Timaeus's fragment should be identified with Myia, as Porphyry suggests, the fact that Pythagoras' daughters were well known and greatly admired is attested as early as the 3rd century BCE. Yet, once again, our sources draw a twofold picture. On the one hand, the Pythagorean women are said to be exceptional. On the other hand, these women stand out as wives, mothers, and daughters.

The list of Pythagorean women our sources mention by name, especially those from Pythagoras' family, is longer than the *Catalogue*. Pythagoras is said to have learnt his doctrines from his sister Theoclea (*Suda* 3124, s.v. Pythagoras).[58] He is occasionally assisted by his mother Pythais in his philosophical endeavours: for example, according to an anecdote reported by Hermippus (Fr. 20 (Wehrli, 1974), in D.L. 8.41), Pythais is responsible for recording and writing down the events during Pythagoras' descent to Hades.[59] Moreover, besides Myia, the available evidence lists three other daughters of Pythagoras and Theano – Arignote,[60] Sara,[61] and Damo[62] – and one granddaughter named Bitale, who later marries Telauges. Specifically, Damo is said to be the one who inherits Pythagoras' unpublished secret

---

[57] Once again, the texts to which Porphyry refers are likely to be the pseudepigraphic letters circulating in the 3rd century CE under Myia's name (see Section 3.1).

[58] This is more likely to be a misreading of Aristoxenus' Fr. 15, according to which Pythagoras learns his 'ethical' doctrines from Themistoclea, the prophetess of Apollo in Delphi (*en Delphois*, rather than *adelphēs*, sister). That Themistoclea, or Aristoclea, is Pythagoras' teacher is also recorded by Diogenes (8.8, 21) and Porphyry (*VP* 41). Most likely, the purpose of this anecdote is to portray Pythagoras' wisdom as god-given. There is also a clear link to Socrates, who, according to Plato's *Symposium* (201d), is educated by the Delphic priestess Diotima.

[59] Hermippus' fragment is satirical of Pythagoras' belief in the afterlife. Yet, this account is unlikely to be a complete fabrication and, since Pythais is not the target of Hermippus' criticism, the reference to her participation in Pythagoras' activities may well be relied upon (Burkert, 1972: 102–3). On Pythais as Pythagoras' mother, see also Porph. *VP* 2; Iamb. *VP* 4. The only other piece of information available about Pythais is that she was originally called Parthenis and that she changed her name and called her son Pythagoras because his birth was announced by the Pythia, the oracle of Apollo in Delphi (Iamb. *VP* 7). In the Early Academy, Pythagoras is believed to be the son of Apollo. This claim is attributed to Epimenides, Eudoxus, and Xenocrates, and rejected by Iamblichus (*VP* 7–8). Once again, the connection with Apollo depicts Pythagoras as divine. Moreover, the same is said of Plato's mother, Perictione (D.L. 3.2 – see Section 3.2.2). For further evidence on Pythagoras' parents, see Demand (1973).

[60] Arignote is mentioned by Porphyry (*VP* 4, quoted earlier in this section), who suggests that she might have left written works. The *Suda* introduces her as a philosopher, a disciple of Pythagoras, rather than his daughter, and the author of philosophical and religious writings (3872, s.v. Arignote – see also Clem. *Strom.* 4.19.121).

[61] The only evidence for Sara is an anonymous *Life of Pythagoras* quoted by Photius (438b). The pseudepigraphic treatise *On Human Nature* is ascribed to a woman named Aesara, which might be linked to Pythagoras' daughter. Thesleff, however, ascribes this treatise to a Pythagorean man named Aresas (1965: 48.21). This attribution is discussed further in Section 3.2.1.

[62] In the *Suda*, Pythagoras is said to have a son named Damon rather than a daughter (3120, s.v. Pythagoras).

notes, which she, in turn, passes on to her daughter Bitale (D.L. 8.42; Iamb. *VP* 146).[63] The fact that Pythagoras anecdotally leaves his works to his daughter and granddaughter rather than his son shows that the Pythagorean women are invaluable to the community: Damo, for example, faithfully abides by the Pythagorean vow of silence and is trusted to preserve Pythagoras' original teachings. However, this also suggests that these women's activities are primarily confined to the domestic sphere and ultimately remain private.[64] The anecdotes reiterate the image of women having a role in philosophy only insofar as they transmit and facilitate male knowledge: Pythais assists her son in enquiring into the soul and afterlife, and Damo is the keeper of her father's memoirs. Either way, women are auxiliaries and serve the purpose of circulating men's ideas rather than their own. Women hold an honoured status within a constricted domestic role. Two possible exceptions to this picture are a fragment about the Pythagorean Timycha and some sayings ascribed to Theano in the Hellenistic period.

2.2.3 The Pythagorean Women as Philosophical Champions

The first name the author of the *Catalogue* includes among the most famous Pythagorean women is Timycha, wife of Myllias the Crotonian. The same name is cited elsewhere in the *Lives*, once by Porphyry (*VP* 61) and twice by Iamblichus (*VP* 189–94, 214). Evidence for this comes from the 3rd-century historians Neanthes and Hippobotus.[65] Porphyry's account is incomplete. Iamblichus presents Timycha as the paradigmatic example of Pythagorean temperance and courage.

While she is in the final stages of pregnancy, travelling with her husband from Tarentum to Metapontum, Timycha is ambushed and taken prisoner by the tyrant Dionysius of Syracuse.[66] Iamblichus writes that she tries to escape but

---

[63] The source for this is an apocryphal letter ascribed to Lysis and addressed to Hipparchus, or Hippasus, who is admonished because unlike Damo he made Pythagoras' doctrines public (Thesleff, 1965: 111.14–114.12). In the 1st century BCE, Alexander Polyhistor published a spurious work entitled *Pythagorean Notes (hypomnēmata)*, which had been in circulation since the 3rd century (Centrone, 2014: 317), and an excerpt of which is quoted by Diogenes (8.24–33). Most likely, then, the purpose of Lysis' letter and Damo's story is to guarantee the authenticity of the *Notes* and ascribe them to Pythagoras himself.

[64] After quoting Lysis' letter, Diogenes adds that Damo kept the doctrines secret 'despite being a woman'. Like Timycha in the next section, she is not subject to faults and vices that were considered specifically female. See Montepaone (1993: 80–2); Taylor (2006: 221).

[65] Hippobotus is a Greek historian of philosophy, author of *On Philosophical Sects* and *List of Philosophers*, often cited by Diogenes (1.19, 42).

[66] This is not the only time Dionysius tries to infiltrate the Pythagorean circles. Aristoxenus writes that Dionysius had also imprisoned the Pythagoreans Damon and Phintias, requesting to be included in their community (Fr. 31). See also Porph. *VP* 60–1; Iamb. *VP* 233–6.

cannot move past a field of beans.[67] To avoid revealing Pythagorean secrets to Dionysius, then, Timycha cuts her tongue off.

> 'But you shall go free with appropriate escort,' Dionysius said, 'if you teach me one thing only.' Myllias asked what he wanted to learn, and Dionysius said: 'Just this, for what reason your friends chose to die rather than to trample on beans.' And Myllias immediately replied: 'They submitted to death to avoid trampling on beans, whereas I would rather trample on beans to avoid telling you the reason for this.' Dionysius was astonished and ordered to take him away and torture Timycha, thinking that being a woman, pregnant, without her husband, and in fear of torture she would blab more easily. The noble woman gnashed her teeth, bit her tongue off, and spat it at the tyrant, showing that, even if her female nature were to be overcome by tortures and forced to reveal the secrets, the thing that serves that purpose would be cut off.
>
> (Neanthes *FGrHist* 84 Frs. 31a-b, in Iamb. *VP* 189–94)

The fragment is anecdotal. Biting off one's tongue as a sign of courage is a recurring theme in ancient philosophical doxography.[68] Nevertheless, this anecdote gives an inkling of Pythagorean way of life and education. Dionysius' goal is to have Timycha and Myllias divulge Pythagoras' secret teachings and, specifically, the reason behind the Pythagorean avoidance of beans. That the disciples are forbidden from eating beans is a generally known and yet inexplicable tenet of ancient Pythagoreanism.[69] To abide by this prohibition, Timycha and Myllias refuse to cross the bean field and are captured by Dionysius. Moreover, to keep these teachings secret Myllias refuses to speak to Dionysius, and Timycha allegedly goes as far as to bite off her own tongue. As a result, both Timycha and her husband Myllias abide by two key Pythagorean rules: the ban against beans and the vow of silence. Noteworthy is that the tyrant considers Timycha more likely to break because she is a woman and because she is pregnant. The Pythagorean

---

[67] The same story is told about Pythagoras himself by Diogenes on the evidence of Hermippus (8.39–40).

[68] Diogenes tells the same story about Zeno of Elea (9.26–27) and Anaxarchus (9.58–59). In *On Talkativeness*, Plutarch also mentions the Athenian courtesan Leaena, who kept silent on the conspiracy against the tyrants Hippias and Hipparchus and was commemorated with a statue of a tongue-less lioness (505d-f – see also Ath. 13.596f).

[69] For example, Pythagoras is reputed to have talked an ox out of eating beans (Porph. *VP* 24; Iamb. *VP* 61). Aristotle links this taboo to sexual regulations, as beans resemble human genitalia and smell like semen (Fr. 195). According to Clement, they cause infertility (*Strom.* 3.24.1–2). Diogenes, again on the evidence of Aristotle, suggests that beans resemble the jointless gates of Hades (8.34 – see also Pliny, *Natural History* 18.30), which might connect this taboo with Pythagoras' teachings on the afterlife. Porphyry claims that beans are to be avoided as they spring from the earth, which is the ultimate origin of all things (*VP* 44). Iamblichus believes that Pythagoras suffers from favism (*VP* 106). By contrast, Aristoxenus denies that the Pythagoreans follow such a rule to begin with (Fr. 25). For a discussion of the ban, see Riedweg (2005: 68–71).

Timycha, then, succeeds in doing what pregnant women were considered unable to do: she is courageous and self-controlled.

This anecdote suggests that some women are introduced to Pythagoras' secret doctrines alongside men and that there are at least some aspects of the Pythagorean way of life, such as silence and diet, men and women implement in the same way. Despite the scantiness of reliable information, then, there are three preliminary conclusions we can draw from the evidence analysed in this section. First, women are admitted both to Pythagoras' public lectures and into his community of disciples. Second, women are primarily lectured on family relationships and in accordance with their traditional domestic roles as wives, mothers, and daughters. Nevertheless, and third, some of Pythagoras' teachings are targeted to both male and female disciples. If Neanthes is right in reporting that at least some Pythagorean women abide by the same rules as their fellow Pythagorean men, such as the vow of silence and eating habits, what makes these women true Pythagoreans goes beyond their domestic roles. These women, too, live a Pythagorean way of life.

Further evidence for the Pythagorean women as moral *exempla* comes from the Hellenistic precepts ascribed to Theano. Later sources portray Theano as an intellectual authority. In the 2nd century CE, Clement describes Theano as the first woman to devote herself to philosophy and produce written works (*Strom.* 1.80.4).[70] Moreover, she is the only woman Diogenes includes in the list of famous Pythagoreans, whose lives are worth recording (8.50). This suggests that Theano holds a prominent place not only among the Pythagorean women but also among the Pythagoreans more generally. The 3rd-century grammarian Censorinus, author of *On Birthday*, cites her as the Pythagorean authority on the question of whether women can give birth after seven months of pregnancy (5.7). Finally, the 10th-century Byzantine encyclopaedia *Suda* 83–84 ascribes four treatises to Theano, Brotinus' wife – *Pythagorean Sayings*, or *Apophtegms* (*apophthegmata*), *Women's Exhortations*, *On Virtue*, and *On Pythagoras* – and three works to Theano the wife of Pythagoras – *Philosophical Notes*, *Sayings*, and an untitled poem.

Some of the sayings attributed to Theano are collected by Hellenistic and post-Hellenistic scholars. Most of them contribute to the image of Theano as the ideal wife. For example, Clement writes that, after being complimented on her beautiful arm, Theano replied that it was not public property (*Strom.* 4.19.121.2–3).[71]

---

[70] Further 2nd-century evidence for the reception of Theano as a Pythagorean sage comes from Lucian of Samosata (*Amores* 30, *Images* 18–19).

[71] The same maxim is collected in Plutarch's *Advice to the Bride and Groom* (142c11-13) and by Stobaeus (4.23.49). For a detailed analysis of Theano's sayings, see Dutsch (2020: 71–114). Dutsch compares the sayings with the Hellenistic *chreiai* – that is, anecdotes about

Diogenes says that she would lecture her fellow Pythagoreans on marital relationships advising them against infidelity and urging them to bring offerings to the
gods after laying with their husbands (D.L. 8.43).[72] And Stobaeus records Theano
claiming that what makes her famous is her loom and marital bed (4.23.32), that
a woman's duty is 'to please her husband' (4.23.55), and that an unbridled horse is
more trustworthy than a woman without reason (*Flor.* 268). Yet three anecdotes
paint a different picture and, as such, deserve special attention: Theano is also
believed to have lectured her pupils about the afterlife ('Life would be a feast for
the wicked if the soul were not immortal', Clem. *Strom.* 4.7.44.2),[73] the value of
silence ('In the matters of which it is honourable to speak, it is shameful to keep
silent, and if it is shameful to speak, it is honourable to keep silent', Stob. *Flor.*
269),[74] and the definition of love as 'an emotion of an unoccupied soul' (270).
The suggestion is that our sources do not exclusively picture Theano as a female
expert on the private sphere. Rather, she is occasionally portrayed as a well-
rounded philosopher. Most of her precepts target women, but at least three of
them are of interest to both men and women.

The following should be noted. First, and most importantly, there is no earlier
evidence to support the attribution of these sayings to Theano in the 5th century.
Most likely, these are all later maxims ascribed to a famous female sage from the
past and cannot be used as evidence of the content of Theano's original
teachings. Rather, the maxims are the first evidence of the reception of the
Pythagorean women in the Hellenistic and post-Hellenistic periods. This leads
us to the next remark. As I noted at the beginning of Section 2.2, the available
evidence for Pythagorean women can be organised into three groups: the 4th-
and 3rd-century reports about Pythagoras' teaching women and welcoming

---

famous characters from the past giving brief responses and moral advice to unnamed
interlocutors, which were used as rhetorical and pedagogical exercises. This suggests that
these witty sayings are examples of Hellenistic rather than Presocratic wisdom.
Nonetheless, they portray Theano as an authority.

[72] Iamblichus attributes the same maxim to a woman named Deino and married to Brotinus
(*VP* 132) and adds that these women later persuaded Pythagoras to deliver the same
teachings, as evidenced by the Crotonian speech (55). Given the connection of Theano
to Brotinus in the doxography, Deino is most likely to be a misreading for Theano
(Taylor, 2006: 180). The same maxim is reported by Stobaeus (4.23.53) and Clement
(*Strom.* 4.19.121.3–4). For a discussion of this apophthegm, see Montepaone (1993: 97–
8). In the same passage, Theano is also credited with saying that, in the company of
their husbands, women should take off their shame and clothes, which is 'that in virtue
of which (one is) called a woman'. Pomeroy takes this to suggest that for Theano and
the Pythagoreans beyond social costumes male and female natures are the same
(2013: 6). This interpretation is criticised by Brodersen (2014).

[73] Clement links this to a similar claim by Plato in the *Phaedo* (107c5-8), fabricating the hypothesis
that Theano was Plato's original source.

[74] A similar maxim is ascribed to Pythagoras himself (Stob. 3.34.7.2). On the immortality of the
soul and silence as specifically Pythagorean topics, see Montepaone (2011: 16–7).

women in his cohorts of disciples, the sayings attributed to Theano in 1st-century sources, and the pseudepigrapha. I shall consider the latter group in the next section. For the time being, I argue that the biographies and the sayings draw a twofold picture. On the one hand, Theano is singled out for being Pythagoras' wife and the mother of his children. On the other hand, she is portrayed as a wise woman and a teacher. In turn, the maxims can be divided into two groups: most sayings draw the picture of Theano as an exemplary wife, who is wise insofar as she is an expert on women's issues and teaches women how to behave with their husbands and families. These anecdotes convey the traditional view of women as faithful wives devoted to their spouses. Yet a few sayings show that Theano is also seen as an authority on a greater variety of subjects, both gendered and genderless, such as the nature of the soul. Like Timycha, then, Theano becomes a philosophical champion.

2.3 Preliminary Conclusions

My first task has been to determine what kind of sages the early Pythagorean women might have been and how, if at all, they contributed to the unfolding of Pythagoreanism in its earliest stages and the development of the community. Scholars have proposed two ways to explain why Pythagoras turns his attention to the education of women and, as Rowett writes, includes women in his intellectual project: the belief in the reincarnation of souls and the way of life.[75] The Pythagoreans are known for believing that at death the soul transmigrates into another body and that, consequently, all ensouled beings are somewhat akin and interconnected parts of the same life cycle (Dicaearchus Fr. 33, in Porph. *VP* 19). This affects the way the Pythagoreans live their everyday life: for example, they arguably refuse to kill and eat animals that share with humans the feature of being ensouled (D.L. 8.13; Iamb. *VP* 85, 108, 168–9). Similarly, Xenophanes mocks Pythagoras for not beating a puppy whose howling reminded him of the soul of his departed friend (D.L. 8.36). Finally, Pythagoras is even anecdotally reputed to have taught a bear not to harm other animals and an ox not to eat beans just as he would have done with his

---

[75] The inclusion of women has also been linked to the Pythagorean notion of harmony and specifically to the need to create harmonious unity between the wider community and private households. For example, Nails writes that the Pythagorean texts ascribed to and about women draw a link between being a good citizen and a good family member (1989) and Haskins argues that they show the interdependence between the public and the private sphere (2005: 319). On the idea that the education of women is aimed at harmonising city and household, see also Munier (1932: 12–20); Izzi (2009: 207); Harper (in Warren, 2009: 78–90); Warren (2009: 63–7). However, I find no evidence that this is how the early Pythagoreans approached gender and gender relations. In contrast, that city and family should be in concord is made explicit in the pseudepigrapha. See, for example, Aesara's *On Human Nature* in Section 3.2.1.

pupils (Porph. *VP* 23–4; Iamb. *VP* 60–1). The suggestion is that the belief in reincarnation informs the way the Pythagoreans treat and train non-human animals. Women, too, have souls. For example, according to the Peripatetic biographers Dicaearchus (Fr. 36) and Clearchus (Fr. 10),[76] Pythagoras himself would claim that he had once lived as a courtesan named Alco. If so, the belief that men and women are fellow ensouled beings might have influenced the way Pythagoras treated and educated his female followers.

Alternatively, and more likely in my view, the inclusion of women has been linked to the way of life. According to Plato's *Republic*, Pythagoras is an influential teacher and the founder of a philosophical way of life (see Section 2.1). His followers are distinguished by their singular lifestyle and behaviour. The limited evidence available for the Pythagorean way of life – namely, the Crotonian speeches and, most importantly, the *akousmata* – target both men and women. Specifically, the teachings are about domestic life and religious rituals and, as such, are addressed to a female audience. Yet a few maxims, such as the ban against eating beans and that against making the doctrines public, seem to be followed by both male and female disciples. Therefore, women are an integral part of Pythagoras' intellectual project insofar as they practise a way of life informed by Pythagorean doctrines. Not only would the Pythagorean women live as they are taught, but, as the evidence for Theano and Myia suggests, some of them may also have been teachers themselves. Thus, a woman becomes a Pythagorean by living like one, and she lives like a Pythagorean both in private with her husband and the members of her household and in public with her fellow Pythagoreans.

Overall, the evidence for ancient Pythagoreanism, and specifically the fragments by Antisthenes, Dicaearchus, and Aristoxenus, show that women play a prominent role in the communities and are unusually educated, both as audiences of Pythagoras' open lectures and as part of his select following. Most women receive a female-specific education on domestic topics, with special focus on the husband–wife relationship. As Timaeus writes, the Pythagoreans excel as women among women. Yet Neanthes' anecdote about Timycha avoiding beans and refusing to spill the Pythagorean secrets suggests that some precepts were implemented by men and women alike – or that some women lived according to the same teachings as their husbands.

The 4th- and 3rd-century historians and biographers ascribe no philosophical ideas to the early Pythagorean women. Nonetheless, from the Hellenistic period onwards, Theano becomes the mouthpiece for ethical teachings and

---

[76] The source for the Peripatetic fragments is Wehrli (1974). Both Dicaearchus and Clearchus are quoted in Aulus Gellius' *Attic Nights* (4.11.14).

philosophical maxims. Again, whilst most sayings focus on women-related questions, there is also evidence of Theano teaching about the immortality of the soul. Therefore, the teachings Pythagoras delivered to women in the 5th century are primarily but not only about family life. The women are also the recipients of more general Pythagorean wisdom. Similarly, the sayings ascribed to Theano are primarily, but not only directed at wives. Some of them also tackle broader ethical and psychological questions. If I am right, the first role women play in Pythagorean societies is a relatively traditional one. Nevertheless, being admitted into the community and adopting the lifestyle might have opened the door to the possibility of engaging further with Pythagorean thought. We have started to build up the picture of the Pythagorean woman as a twofold sage, both an expert of the household and a well-rounded intellectual. Next, I examine whether, and if so how, this is echoed in the pseudepigrapha.

3 Late Pythagoreanism: Writers, Pseudepigraphers, and Philosophers

The second part of this Element focuses on the Pythagorean female sage in the Hellenistic and post-Hellenistic periods. Our sources of evidence are the letters and treatises written between the 2nd century BCE and the 2nd century CE and ascribed to Pythagorean women. These were edited and collected in Thesleff's *The Pythagorean Texts of the Hellenistic Period* (1965).

3.1 The Pythagorean Pseudepigrapha

The Pythagorean women are credited with writing ten letters – eight of which are ascribed to Theano, the alleged wife of Pythagoras – and five treatises. Most letters consist of woman-to-woman advice about family life: Theano writes to Euboule urging her not to raise children in luxury (Thesleff 195.22–196.34), to Eurydice showing her how to react to her husband's affair and comparing women to musical instruments (197.12–24),[77] to Callisto on how to manage the members of the household with authority and self-restraint (197.25–198.28),[78] to Nicostrate again concerning her husband's infidelity (198.29–200.15),[79] and to Timareta arguably about household managing

---

[77] Although the comparison of wives with melodic instruments and courtesans with shepherd's pipes is quite general, Pomeroy interprets this as an allusion to Pythagorean musical theory (2013: 82).

[78] Archytas of Tarentum was known for being merciful and exercising self-restraint towards his slaves: in a fragment by Aristoxenus, he refuses to act out of anger and punish them (Fr. 30, in Iamb. *VP* 197–8). However, Theano's letter is too general to establish a connection with this anecdote.

[79] As mentioned earlier, the 5th-century Pythagoras and Theano were known for forbidding their pupils from being unfaithful to their spouses (see Sections 2.2.1–2.2.3). In the pseudepigrapha,

(200.26–29).[80] Similarly, Myia writes to Phillys urging her to raise her children with moderation (115–6), and Melissa to Cleareta against women's luxurious clothing (115.24–116.17). The last three letters are simple personal messages from the authors to their interlocutors on various and not noticeably philosophical topics: Theano writes to the doctor Euclides enquiring about his health (196.35–197.11), to Rhodope lending her a copy of Plato's *Parmenides* (200.16–25),[81] and to Timonides asking to put an end to their quarrel (200.30–5).

The treatises, on the other hand, include more general arguments and theories. They can be divided into two groups: the ethical and the theoretical texts. The ethical treatises are *On the Moderation of Women*, which is attributed to Phintys the Spartan (Stob. 4.23.61; Thesleff 151.14–154.11), and *On the Harmony of Women*, ascribed to Perictione (Stob. 4.28.19; Thesleff 142.14–146.22). These texts focus on female morality and virtues: as detailed in Section 3.2.2, the former argues that men and women have the same virtues, but moderation is a preferably female form of excellence; the latter encourages women to develop all virtues, including intelligence, courage, and justice, as well as moderation. The theoretical treatises are *On Piety*, ascribed to Theano, *On Wisdom*, ascribed to Perictione, and *On Human Nature*, ascribed to Aesara.[82] In *On Piety*, the author challenges the Aristotelian interpretation of the Pythagorean belief that numbers are the principles of all things: unlike Aristotle, according to whom this meant that things come to be from numbers, Theano interprets the saying to mean that things come to be according to numbers, for once the cosmos is ordered everything in it can be numbered (Stob. 1.10.13; Thesleff 195). Perictione argues that the purpose of wisdom is the contemplation of all existing things, which makes philosophy superior to the other sciences (Stob. 3.1.120–1; Thesleff 146.1–22). Finally, *On Human Nature* focuses on the structure of the soul and argues that its orderly arrangement

---

however, the focus is on women putting up with their husbands' mistresses, rather than on refraining from extramarital affairs. The treatise *On the Harmony of Women* explicitly acknowledges this double-standard ('This fault is permitted to men, but to women never', Thesleff 144.12–14), which seems alien to 5th-century Pythagoreanism.

[80] The only surviving fragment quoted in a 2nd-century dictionary by Julius Pollux is ' . . . master and mistress of the house . . . ' (*Onom.* 10.21).

[81] Notably, this confirms that the letters are post-Platonic and written either by a woman named after Theano or under Theano's pseudonym, but not by the wife of Pythagoras herself.

[82] It should be noted that most scholars, like Thesleff, distinguish the author of *On the Harmony of Women*, who uses the Ionic dialect with occasional Dorisms, and whom they name Perictione I, from the author of *On Wisdom*, who uses the Doric and is referred to as Perictione II. Similarly, since the prose in Theano's letters differs from *On Piety*, scholars distinguish Theano I and Theano II and attribute the treatise to the former and the letters to the latter. See Thesleff (1961: 113–4); Waithe (1987: 41); Pomeroy (2013: xiii-iv). *Contra* Lambropoulou (1995: 133); Plant (2004: 68–9). On Aesara, Phintys, and Perictione, see Sections 3.2.1–3.2.3.

provides a standard of justice for both the household and the city (Stob. 1.49.27; Thesleff 48.20–50.23). It should be mentioned that, whilst the ethical treatises are attributed to female writers beyond any doubt, the authorship *On Wisdom* and *On Nature* is more contested. I discuss this further in the next sections.

These last two texts are not traditionally included in the list of pseudepigrapha: a fragment on the soul ascribed to Theano and a treatise on Pythagorean harmonics by Ptolemais of Cyrene. As mentioned in the previous section, like her husband, Theano is reputed to have lectured her pupils on the afterlife. Clement says: 'Theano the Pythagorean *writes* that, if the soul were not immortal, life would be a feast for the wicked' (*Strom.* 4.7.44.2, emphasis added). This suggests that what Clement is quoting is not a saying but rather a fragment from a text ascribed to Theano. However, this fragment is not part of Thesleff's edition of the Pythagorean pseudepigrapha. On the other hand, Thesleff includes two excerpts from Ptolemais' treatise on harmonics, quoted by Porphyry's commentary on Ptolemy's *Harmonics* (22.2–24.6; Thesleff 242.10–243.22). In the surviving fragments, Ptolemais compares the Pythagorean music theory with Aristoxenus'. Yet this text should not be counted among the Pythagorean apocrypha as Ptolemais is not a pseudonym: she is a Peripatetic woman writing about Pythagoreanism, rather than a Pythagorean woman, or a Pythagorean pseudepigrapher, herself.[83] Notably, this shows that in the first century, there are women writers and intellectuals.

Thus far, the scholarship on the Pythagorean pseudepigrapha has focused on two questions: (1) *when* and *where* these texts are written, and (2) *by whom*. Specifically, in the case of the pseudepigrapha ascribed to Pythagorean women, the debate is on whether they are written by male or female authors. The issue I investigate in Section 3.2, in contrast, is *what* the texts are about.[84] I briefly review the scholarship on the Pythagorean pseudepigrapha with special focus on dating and pseudonymity issues. I show that the gender debate has acted as a barrier to the engagement with the content and arguments in the texts ascribed to the Pythagorean women. I then leave the debate aside and turn to the philosophical analysis of the pseudepigrapha. Once again, I unpack this into two questions: What, if anything, makes the texts philosophical? And what kind of philosophers do the Pythagorean women turn out to be?

---

[83] On Ptolemais, see Barker (2014). Pomeroy includes the treatise among the women's pseudepigrapha (2013: 95–8).

[84] Other scholars who investigated the content of the pseudepigrapha are Centrone (1990; 2014) and Ulacco (2017). These thorough studies, however, do not analyse the texts ascribed to women in detail.

3.1.1 Chronology

As noted in the Introduction, one of the characteristics of the later Pythagorean tradition is the production of apocrypha. This corpus is exceptionally varied in genre, style, and content. The texts are written over a long period of time with no clear chronological boundaries, originate in different places, such as Alexandria and Rome, use several dialects and archaisms, and belong to various literal and philosophical traditions. This makes the exact dating contested and difficult to determine.

The possible ways to classify the texts are twofold: geographically – that is, according to the place in which the texts were written – and chronologically – that is, by dating. In his edition of the pseudepigrapha, Thesleff argues that most texts are the product of the revival of Pythagoreanism in the Hellenistic period and thus date back to the 3rd century BCE. Specifically, Thesleff divides the texts geographically into two groups: the Pythagorean texts 'from the East', written in Alexandria, in Attic or Ionic dialect, and under the names of either Pythagoras or members of Pythagoras' family; and the Pythagorean texts 'from the West', written in Southern Italy, in Doric, by lesser-known Pythagorean authors (1961: 27–9). Most texts ascribed to Pythagorean women are in the latter group, apart from the letters and treatises by Theano, which are among the Pythagorean pseudepigrapha from the East. The only two exceptions to this classification are the letter ascribed to Myia – who is named after the daughter of Pythagoras, but nevertheless uses the Doric dialect and therefore is included in the second group – and the treatise *On the Harmony of Women* ascribed to Plato's mother Perictione – who is not related to Pythagoras but writes in Ionic like pseudo-Theano.

Thesleff's proposal for an early dating has since been rejected. Nowadays, most scholars maintain that the pseudepigrapha were produced between the 1st century BCE and the 1st century CE, which is when they started being mentioned by our sources (Centrone, 2014: 339).[85] In a recent article, Leonid Zhmud has reorganised the pseudepigrapha chronologically into three time periods (2019: 4): the early texts, written between the late 4th and late 2nd century BCE, in Attic or Ionic, and under the names of Pythagoras and his family members; the middle treatises, written around the 1st century BCE, in Doric dialect, and under the names of other real and fictional Pythagoreans, such as Archytas of Tarentum; and the post-Hellenistic texts, written in the 2nd century CE, again under the names of Pythagoras and his relatives. Only the

---

[85] Thesleff himself revised his proposal: after Burkert's objection that the pseudepigrapha should be dated between the 1st century BCE and the 1st century CE, he postponed the dating to the 2nd century BCE (1972: 88–102).

middle texts survive in full and are considered by Zhmud to be philosophically valuable. The Pythagorean women's letters and treatises, however, belong to the third category and are not discussed further in his article.[86]

Waithe and Pomeroy, whose work specifically centres on the women's texts, proposed a further dating, which, however, has been criticised by scholars of Pythagoreanism. Waithe distinguishes three groups (1987: 11–74): the first generation of Pythagorean women, who live in the 5th century BCE and are members of Pythagoras' family, such as his wife Theano, author of *On Piety*, and his daughter Myia; the second generation of women, which includes Perictione, mother of Plato and author of *On the Harmony of Women*; and the late Pythagorean women from the 2nd century BCE.[87] Pomeroy combines Waithe's and Thesleff's classifications (2013: 49): she distinguishes between Eastern and Western texts and then divides the Pythagorean texts 'from the East' into two groups – the works from the early 3rd century BCE, such as the treatises by Theano and Perictione, and later letters – and the Pythagoreans 'from the West' into 3rd-century authors, such as Aesara, and 2nd-century authors such as Myia.

As for the treatises analysed in Section 3.2, most scholars agree with dating them back to the 1st century BCE (Macris 2016). For the purpose of this Element, I shall not discuss the dating issue further.

3.1.2 The Pseudonymity Issue

The Pythagorean pseudepigrapha are written in the Hellenistic and Imperial Age under the authorship of early Pythagorean philosophers. The pseudonymity issue is therefore threefold: first, the texts are not *early*, but rather late forgeries written using archaic language and pseudonyms of famous 5th- and 4th-century Pythagoreans, such as Pythagoras himself, his wife Theano, his disciple Archytas, and other lesser-known figures. Second, these texts are hardly *Pythagorean*. As noted in the Introduction, the aim of the pseudepigrapha is to portray the Pythagoreans as the precursors of Platonism and Aristotelianism. Hence, the texts have very few Pythagorean elements but rather combine distinctively Platonic and Aristotelian theories, arguments, and language. For example, there is no mention of the doctrine of metempsychosis, which is considered one of the cornerstones of ancient Pythagoreanism. Moreover, though many of these texts discuss the pupils' daily lives, the instructions are

---

[86] The sole exception is *On Piety*, which is ascribed to Theano, and which Zhmud would arguably include in the first group of texts.

[87] Waithe distinguishes the original Pythagorean women, such as Theano, the wife of Pythagoras, from the women who in the Hellenistic Age were named after their Pythagorean predecessors, such as Theano, author of the letters.

not as puzzling and unconventional as some of the early *akousmata*. Finally, in the specific case of the pseudepigrapha written under female names, the debate over the identity, dating, and philosophical leanings of the authors has led scholars to challenge their gender and question whether the pseudepigrapha could have in fact been written by *women*. The assumption is that not only are the texts written by late forgers using pseudonyms of early Pythagoreans but they are also written by men using female names.[88]

The most debated issue concerning the Pythagorean women's texts, then, is whether they are in fact authored by female authors or rather men writing under female pseudonyms. As mentioned in the Introduction, we can distinguish those scholars who give more charitable readings of the pseudepigrapha and thus accept female authorship and the more sceptic ones who highlight the issues raised by attributing the pseudepigrapha to women writers.[89]

Among those scholars arguing for female authorship are Mary Ellen Waithe and Sarah Pomeroy. In her *History of Women Philosophers*, Waithe notes that, whilst forgeries are traditionally attributed to illustrious and authoritative figures from the past, the Pythagorean women named in the apocrypha are otherwise unknown. Her conclusion is that the letters should be considered eponymous – that is, written by the named authors (1987: 59–74). My reply to this argument is that, as shown in Section 2.2 of this Element, early Pythagorean women like Theano were well-known and highly regarded in late antiquity and had acquired the reputation of being intellectual authorities. This would make them plausible and effective spokespersons for the pseudepigrapha. Pomeroy, on the other hand, grants the possibility that the texts might be pseudonymous but does not question the gender of the authors. She argues that, since the pseudepigrapha cover topics traditionally associated with the female gender, such as the husband-wife relationship and the management of the household, and explicitly address an audience of women, they are more likely to have been written by women and from a female point of view. According to Pomeroy, the texts show a certain female sympathy, which prompts the assumption that they are the work of women who are named after or writing under the names of their better-known Pythagorean predecessors (2013: 49–53). In Pomeroy's view, the authors can be both women philosophers and pseudepigraphers.[90]

---

[88] See also Pomeroy (2013: 50).

[89] It should be noted that neither Huizenga nor Deslauriers, whose views are discussed later, explicitly argue against the possibility of ascribing these texts to women but rather draw attention to the main methodological difficulties with this attribution.

[90] Some letters, for example, are written in support of women whose husbands have been adulterous, and thus seem to provide 'rare insight into how these wives felt' (Pomeroy, 2013: 60). For further arguments in support of female authorship, see Wider (1986); Nails (1989: 291–7); Plant (2004: 68–91).

Three counterarguments were more recently proposed against the claim that the pseudepigrapha are authored by women. The first issue is that, whilst the available evidence for early Pythagoreanism suggests that the female role in Pythagorean societies was 'unusually large' and women were allowed to receive an education, the pseudepigrapha picture women as loving mothers and faithful wives and relegate the female gender to a traditional role inside the house. This leads to suggestions that the texts might be apologetic and written to reverse the unconventional reputation of the early Pythagorean women (Huizenga, 2013: 44).[91] My reply to this argument is that our evidence for the status of women in early Pythagorean societies is limited and does not explicitly show that their role went much beyond family life. Furthermore, even if these texts had been fabricated with the purpose of reclaiming a more traditional role for Pythagorean women in society, they could still have been written by female authors.

The second objection is by Marguerite Deslauriers, according to whom, since in Greek antiquity the philosophical way of life is considered unsuitable for women, who lack formal education and do not speak in public, these philosophical texts are unlikely to be the work of female authors (2012: 343–5).[92] Deslauriers is right in noticing that ancient Greek philosophy is an almost exclusively male enterprise and therefore succeeds in challenging the claim that the Pythagorean pseudepigraphers are emancipated from family life. Yet this still does not prove that women could not have authored letters and treatises *about* family life. For example, Deslauriers herself allows for the possibility that women may have practised philosophy among themselves in private. This would at least grant that the private letters from Pythagorean teachers to their younger female pupils could be the work of female authors.[93]

Finally, Deslauriers points out that in antiquity, men could choose to write under female pseudonyms, especially when aiming to educate female pupils.[94] Thus, unlike Pomeroy, Deslauriers suggests that it is because the pseudepigrapha are written *for* women and *about* women that they might not have been

---

[91] On the difference between early and late Pythagorean women, see also Lambropoulou (1995); Montepaone and Catarzi (2016). On the apologetic tone of the pseudepigrapha, see Taylor (2006: 182).

[92] To support this claim, Deslauriers cites the case of Hipparchia, who practises philosophy with the support of her husband Crates, the founder of Cynicism (D.L. 6.96–8). For an alternative account of Hipparchia's philosophical activity, see Protopapa-Marneli (forthcoming).

[93] Snyder argues that the personal tone of the Pythagorean letters, especially the ones from Theano to the doctor Euclides and to her peers Rhodope and Timonides, shows that the authors are not pamphleteering and thus gives no reason to think they write under pseudonyms (1991: 113). Similarly, Plant suggests that the choice of topics such as childcare makes a female audience and author more likely (2004: 79).

[94] See also Lefkowitz and Fant (2005: 163).

authored *by* women. My reply to the latter objection is again twofold. First, as
Deslauriers herself notices (2012: 352), in the Hellenistic and Imperial Age it is
less unusual to come across educated women and female teachers.[95] Second,
and most importantly, for female authorship to be credible and for these texts to
function successfully as teaching aids, the readers should at least believe that the
authors could be women and the Pythagoreans giving their names to the
pseudepigrapha were intellectuals. Female pseudonymity depends on women
being considered able to think and write philosophically – even if mostly about
female ethics, domestic virtues, and family life. Regardless of who in fact wrote
them, the pseudepigrapha show that the Pythagoreans are believed to be intel-
lectually inclined women teaching and studying philosophy.

I shall make three conclusive remarks concerning the authorship debate.
First, the very fact that some of the pseudepigrapha target women shows that,
regardless of who the original authors were, women were at least part of the
intended readership of these philosophical texts. For example, the letters have
female addressees and the ethical treatises teach women how to be virtuous in
their daily lives. This shows that the network of the pseudepigrapha includes
women. As Dutsch has recently argued, quite convincingly, this leaves open the
possibility of finding women on the other end of the correspondence. Like their
readers, the authors of the pseudepigrapha, too, could be women (2020: 130).

Second, and more important, the central arguments both for and against
female authorship often depend on the claim that the Pythagorean women's
apocrypha target women and revolve around women-related questions, such as
how to be a good wife and how to run the household. For example, Pomeroy
thinks that, since the writings are centred on women, they are more likely to
have been written by women, whereas Deslauriers argues that the female focus
of the texts could be the reason why their male authors used female pseudonyms. It is worth noting, however, that some of these texts are not about
women. As I show in the next section, treatises like Perictione's *On Wisdom* and
Aesara's *On Human Nature* cover a wider variety of topics, ranging from the
scope of philosophical enquiry to the theory of numbers as first principles and
the tripartition of the soul. Thus, these treatises challenge the claim that in
antiquity women were reputed to be experts only on the female gender. The
problem is that Aesara and Perictione are the two Pythagorean pseudepigraphers whose gender identity has been most frequently called into question:
Thesleff introduces the author of *On Human Nature* as a Pythagorean man
named Aresas (1965: 48.21–50.11 – see Section 3.2.1), and Huffman (2005:
591–8) and Horky (2015: 33–6 – see Section 3.2.3) have argued that the

---

[95] On women teachers in Ancient Egypt, see Bagnall and Cribiore (2006).

surviving fragments of *On Wisdom* should be ascribed to pseudo-Archytas, rather than Plato's mother.[96] I discuss the authorship of these treatises in more detail later in this Element. For the time being, suffice it to say that when using female sympathy as an argument either for or against female authorship, one should acknowledge that the Pythagorean women are also occasionally chosen as the authors of treatises about number theory and letters about Plato's *Parmenides*. Surely, these texts are fewer in number, and the Pythagorean women are mostly credited with writing about the female gender, family life, and female virtues. Nevertheless, it should not be forgotten that there are also pseudepigrapha venturing into psychological, cosmological, epistemological, and metaphysical speculations about the laws of the cosmos, the soul, numbers, and science.

Third, and most importantly, I mentioned that most scholars focus on the issue of whether the letters and treatises are pseudonymous and, specifically, the likelihood of the authors being women. What I hope to have shown is that, so far, no decisive argument that the pseudepigrapha should be ascribed to male authors has been proposed. This alone does not mean that these texts are undoubtedly by women but simply suggests that the authorship question may not be the most valuable starting point for our enquiry. Rather than asking ourselves who wrote the pseudepigrapha, we should wonder what these texts are about, what makes them philosophical, and what original ideas they bring forth. This is the gap I plan to fill in the final section of the Element.

3.2 The Pythagorean Women's Treatises

The focus of this Element is on the Pythagorean women as philosophers. Specifically, this section examines what is philosophical in the Pythagorean women's pseudepigrapha, what their arguments are, and thus what they can tell us about the Pythagorean female sage. The Pythagorean women are reputed to have authored both letters about family life addressed to their female pupils and philosophical treatises. The latter include mostly ethical arguments about women's virtues, but also theoretical views of the soul, human knowledge, the principles of the cosmos, and the sciences. Further and more detailed examples are analysed in Sections 3.2.1–3.2.3.

I focus on four treatises: Aesara's *On Human Nature*, Perictione's *On the Harmony of Women*, Phintys' *On the Moderation of Women*, and Perictione's *On Wisdom*. This is for two reasons: first, as noted in Section 3.1, unlike the letters, the treatises consist of arguments that are seemingly philosophical and

---

[96] It should be noted that at the Oxford 'Women Intellectuals in Antiquity' Symposium in February 2020, Horky argued for the original attribution of *On Wisdom* to Perictione. For further discussion of the authorship issue, see De Cesaris and Pellò (forthcoming).

influenced by the Platonic and Aristotelian traditions. As such, they contribute first-hand to the reception of the Pythagorean women as philosophers.[97] Second, these four treatises have enough similarities in content and style to appear as part of the same tradition within the pseudepigrapha. This suggests that the treatises were addressed to a similar audience and, possibly, that the authors might have been reading each other's works. Scholars refer to this tradition as the Doric corpus. The Doric pseudepigrapha are all quoted almost in full by Stobaeus. They are written in archaic Doric dialect – except for *On Harmony*, which also has some Ionic language – and strategically combine elements of Platonic and Aristotelian theories under the names of ancient and otherwise unknown Pythagoreans.[98] Their doctrines, too, are interrelated and appear to form one single coherent philosophical system whose principles apply to various fields and aspects of the cosmos, from metaphysics, logic, and cosmology to psychology, ethics, politics, and home economics. This system has been analysed by scholars like Bruno Centrone (1990; 2014) and more recently Angela Ulacco (2017), both of whom refer to the women's treatises in passing.[99] In what follows, I propose to complement their studies, analyse the content of the women's treatises, and show how they relate to the other Doric pseudepigrapha and what they add to this philosophical system. I start from the general question of what the good order of the cosmos is and then zoom in on the question of how to define virtue and, specifically, what wisdom is.

3.2.1 Aesara on the Soul, City, and Family Analogy

Centrone argues that the purpose of the Doric pseudepigrapha is to unveil the principles that are at work in the cosmos and systematically shared by all its different domains (2014: 320–1). As such, the very notion of *systema*, system, is central to these treatises. Two fragments that make this goal explicit are *On the Happiness of the Household*, ascribed to Callicras (Fr. 2, in Stob. 4.28.16; Thesleff 103.21–3), and *On Human Nature*, ascribed to the Pythagorean woman Aesara. Both texts show how the same principles apply to various

---

[97] A comprehensive account of the pseudepigrapha should also include a philosophical analysis of the letters written to and arguably by Pythagorean women, which is unfortunately beyond the scope of this Element. The most recent studies are Dutsch (2020: 173–210) and Twomey (forthcoming).

[98] Centrone distinguishes two groups within the pseudepigrapha (2014: 317): those attributed to Pythagoras and the members of his family, such as his wife Theano and daughter Myia, and those written under the pseudonyms of other Pythagoreans, which have a clearer philosophical agenda (see also Zhmud, 2019: 75). The treatises ascribed to Aesara, Phintys, and Perictione belong to the latter group.

[99] Centrone simply mentions the presence of treatises ascribed to women as one of the few 'Pythagoreanising features' of the pseudepigrapha (2014: 333, n. 46).

systems – politics, home economics, and, in the case of Aesara, human psychology.

Before turning to Aesara's treatise, a remark about authorship is in order: as I noted in the previous section, the identity behind *On Human Nature* is a point of lively academic controversy. Stobaeus introduces the author as 'Aesara, a Pythagorean from Lucania' (1.49.27; Thesleff 40.21). One adjective – *leukanēs*, Lucanian – is feminine. For the other word, 'Pythagorean', the manuscript tradition is twofold: according to one version, Stobaeus identifies Aesara as a Pythagorean man (*pythagoreiou*); according to the other version, her name is followed by the patronymic *pythagorou*, '(daughter) of Pythagoras'. As a result, the scholarship is divided into two factions: those who ascribe the treatise to a man and those who identify the author as a Pythagorean woman. Thesleff, for example, takes the author to be male and thus changes Aesara into Aresas, a Pythagorean man mentioned in Iamblichus' *Vita* (266), and *leukanēs* into the masculine *leukanou*.[100] Thesleff justifies the emendation by arguing that the manuscript tradition was influenced by Photius, according to whom Pythagoras had a daughter named Sara (438b), and therefore misinterpreted the name of the author.[101] Further, Thesleff notices that since Aesara is said to be a Lucanian, she is unlikely to be Pythagoras' daughter, who was arguably from Croton. Yet most scholars nowadays tend to follow the manuscript tradition and ascribe the text to a Pythagorean woman named Aesara.[102]

Our first example of a Pythagorean woman philosopher in the Doric pseud-epigrapha, then, is Aesara the metaphysician. Her treatise, *On Human Nature*, revolves around the question of the principle of justice, not only for an individual human but also for the city-state and the household. *On Human Nature* can be divided into four parts: an introductory statement according to which humans have within themselves the same model of justice that applies to the city and the family (Thesleff 48.22–49.3); the theory of the tripartition of the soul (49.3–11); the general definition of harmonious system (49.11–50.7); and the application of this general model of justice to the soul (50.7–23).

> The human nature seems to me to be a standard of law and justice for both the household and the city. For by following on the tracks within themselves and searching, people would discover that within themselves lie law and justice,

---

[100] See also Centrone, 1990: 181.   [101] On Pythagoras' family, see Section 2.2.2.

[102] See Allen, 1985: 151; Waithe, 1987: 19–29; Plant, 2004: 81; Taylor, 2006: 242; Pomeroy, 2013: 99–102. This was also the case for Gilles Ménage (1984: 12). Brown even changes the name of the author into Arignote, another daughter of Pythagoras who is reputed to have left written works (*Suda* 3872, s.v. Arignote; Clem. *Strom.* 4.19.121; Porph. *VP* 4). For a detailed analysis of the debate and further bibliographical references, see Migliorati (2020).

which is the orderly arrangement of the soul. ... A system of community could neither arise out of one thing only nor out of many similar things (for since things are different, it is necessary that the parts of the soul within ourselves are also different, just as is the case of sight, hearing, taste, and smell in the body, for not all things have the same harmonious relation to each other); nor (could the system arise) out of things that are many and different – especially those that are at random – but out of things that are crafted for the fulfilment, order, and harmony of the whole system. ... For if they had an equal share of both power and honour, despite being unequal – some worse, others better, and others in the middle – the community of parts could not be harmonised throughout the soul; and if they had an unequal share, and the worse, rather than the better, had the greater share, there would be much unreason and disorder in the soul; and if the better had the greater share, the worse the lesser share, and each of these not in relation to reason, there could not be unanimity, friendship, and justice in the soul, since when each thing is arranged in relation to a reason that is in harmony, I say that this kind of thing is justice. Indeed, a certain unanimity and agreement accompanies such an arrangement. This sort of thing could justly be called good law of the soul, whichever, due to the better part ruling and the worse part being ruled, adds the strength of virtue. Friendship, love, and friendliness, being cognate and kindred, will sprout from these parts. (Stob. 1.49.27; Thesleff 48.21–50.11)

The treatise introduces the notion of *systema* by arguing that the same standard of law and justice applies to an individual human, her city, and her home. As such, in the Doric pseudepigrapha the traditional Platonic parallelism between city and human soul, or nature, is broadened to include the household (*oikos*), women, and the family. In the individual, public, and private spheres, the standard of justice is identified with the orderly arrangement of the whole and its parts.[103] According to Aesara, such good arrangement of the whole should meet three conditions: first, the whole, or system, should have parts ('The *systema* of commonality could not come to be from one thing only'). That the whole has different parts is supported with an analogy between the soul and the body, which has different organs and senses.[104] The second condition is that the parts should be different ('Nor could it arise from many similar things'). Finally, the parts should not be arranged at random but 'in accordance with the fulfilment, order, and harmony of the whole'. For things to be in harmony, each thing should have its own share of power (*dynamis*), different things should have different shares and, most importantly, superior things should have a greater share than the inferior. This brings about a state of

---

[103] Such good order (*diakosmasis*) is also mentioned in Euryphamus' *On Life* (Stob. 4.39.21; Theselff 86.11) and Hippodamus' *On Happiness* (Stob. 4.39.26; Thesleff 96.27–8).

[104] For further arguments by analogy, especially with sense organs, see Phintys' *On Moderation* and Perictione's *On Wisdom* in Sections 3.2.2–3.2.3.

concord, friendship, and again justice: an ordered soul, city, or household is a harmonious soul, city, or household, which in turn makes it just and virtuous.

A *systema*, then, is a complex structure whose numerous dissimilar parts abide by the same principles and rules and are thus fitted together in harmony. According to Aesara, family, city, and soul abide by the same general rule of justice and virtue, which states that superior things should be in control of the others. This is then applied to the particular case of the soul and its three parts.

> For by following on the tracks within themselves and searching, people would discover that within themselves lie law and justice, which is the orderly arrangement of the soul. For being threefold, (the soul) is constructed with three functions: (the mind) for thought and intelligence, (the spirit) for strength and power, and desire for love and friendliness. And thus, these are all arranged in relation to one another, so that the best part of the soul is in command, the worst is ruled, and the middle holds the middle place, both ruling and being ruled. God thus crafted these things in accordance with reason in the modelling and completion of the human body, as the human alone, and none of the other mortal animals, is considered to be a recipient of law and justice. ... The mind inspects and tracks its objects, spirit adds impulse and strength to the inspections; and desire, being akin to affection, fits together with the mind. ... The mind can harmonise these things with it, becoming delightsome through education and virtue.
>
> (Stob. 1.49.27; Thesleff 49.1–50.23)

In the first section of the treatise, Aesara distinguishes three parts based on their functions (*erga*, what they do):[105] mind, or intellect (*nous*), for thought, or judgement (*gnōmē*), and intelligence, or practical wisdom (*phronēsis*), spirit (*thumos*) for strength (*alkē*) and ability, or power (*dynamis*), and desire (*epithumia*) for love (*erōs*) and kindliness (*philophrosynē*). Next, mind is described as the superior part in control of the others. This is for two reasons: first, spirit and desire are said to collaborate with the *nous* ('Spirit adds impulse and strength to the inspections, and desire fits together with the mind'); second, at the end of the treatise mind is said to be capable of keeping things in order and harmony. Notably, this leads Aesara to argue that humans alone provide a standard of justice and good order for the city and the family. Humans are prioritised over other living beings in virtue of their ability to think and inspect, and thus

---

[105] The predilection of triadic divisions is a recurring feature of the pseudepigrapha and, according to Centrone, one of the few early Pythagorean elements in the *corpus* (2014: 333). For further examples of tripartitions in the Pythagorean women's texts, see *On Moderation* and *On Wisdom* below. For triadic divisions in 5th-century Pythagoreanism, see Ar. *On the Heavens* 1.1.268a10-13; Porph. *VP* 51; Iamb. *VP* 152. These passages are analysed in Betegh (2014: 159–66).

recreate the harmonious arrangement of their soul at home and in public affairs. Humans alone are crafted to embody the virtue of justice.[106]

The model is Plato's *Republic* and his theory of the tripartite soul. Plato too draws parallels between the city, on the one hand, and the individual soul, on the other, and shows that they both abide by the same criterion of justice (2.368 c-69b, 4.434d-5 c, 4.440e-1). Both the city and the soul are organised into three classes, or parts, each with its own function and the relative excellence, or virtue.[107] The highest class are the guardians, whose virtue is wisdom (*sophia*, 4.427d-9a, 4.441e-2b), and who correspond to the rational part of the soul (4.438e-9d); next are the soldiers, whose virtue is courage (*andreia*, 4.429a-30 c, 4.442b-c), and who correspond to the spirited part of the soul (4.439e-40a); and the lowest class are the workers, whose virtue is moderation (*sōphrosynē*, 4.430d-1d, 4.442 c-d), and who correspond to the desiderative part of the soul (4.438e-9d). The state in which each part of the soul and each member of the city – 'the strongest, the weakest, and those in the middle' (4.432a) – plays its role at best is described as harmonious (4.431 c-2e, 4.443e). Justice, in turn, comes about when each component 'does its job and does not meddle in the business of others' (4.433a). In *On Human Nature*, then, Aesara borrows Plato's definition of justice as 'to each one's own' (4.433a-4 c, 4.441d-e, 4.443 c-d). Yet not only does the treatise apply this principle to the city and the soul, but also to the family and the household.

In conclusion, the following should be noted: Aesara's treatise concerns human nature in general. If the manuscript tradition is right in identifying the author as a Pythagorean woman, this is an example of a female author who philosophises generally about the parts of the soul and the order of the cosmos, city, and household, rather than an expert of the household writing about women and women-related matters.

3.2.2 Perictione and Phintys on Virtue

In *On Human Nature*, the soul is organised into three parts, each having a specific function. Nothing is said about the specific virtues of each part. Aesara more generally writes that the organisation of mind, spirit, and desire, with the former taking the lead over the latter, brings about justice. Overlapping claims about harmony and virtue are made in the treatise *On the Harmony of*

---

[106] For a similar cosmological claim, according to which human beings are created and endowed with wisdom by a god, or demiurge, in accordance with reason, see Perictione's *On Wisdom* below.

[107] For the functionalist account of *aretē*, virtue, as excellence at performing one's *ergon*, job, which seems to be implied in Aesara's treatise, see Phintys' *On the Moderation of Women* and Perictione's *On Wisdom* below.

Women, ascribed to the Pythagorean Perictione.[108] The treatise revolves around the question of what makes women harmonious. The answer is that a woman is to be called harmonious when she is full of virtues.

The treatise survives in two fragments. The first fragment is divided into two parts: a more general ethical statement about what it means for women to be harmonious and virtuous, which is quoted after this paragraph, and more specific advice on how to be virtuous in their everyday domestic life (Thesleff 143.1–145.6). The second fragment focuses on the care for parents (Stob. 4.25.50; Thesleff 145.7–26).[109] The introductory theory of virtue is the following:

> We should think that the harmonious woman is full of both intelligence and moderation, for the soul must be truly in full possession of virtue so that she will be just, courageous, intelligent, and beautified with self-sufficiency and despising empty opinion. For from these virtues good deeds happen to a woman for both herself and her husband, and again her children, house, and perhaps also city, if such women were to govern cities or people, as we see in monarchies. (Fr. 1, in Stob. 4.28.19; Thesleff 142.18–143.1)

This fragment can be analysed into two steps: the definition of 'harmonious woman' (Thesleff 142.18–21) and the explanation of why women ought to be harmonious (142.21–143.1). A woman is harmonious when she has both intelligence (*phronēsis*) and moderation (*sōphrosynē*). Being fully virtuous in turn also makes her just (*dikaia*) and courageous (*andreia*). The reason why women should achieve such fullness of virtue is that it benefits both the woman herself and her house, family, and city. Again, the human, the household, and the wider society are all held together under the same standard of excellence and harmony.[110] Perictione, thus, is credited with two claims: first, being harmonious means being in full possession of all virtues, intelligence, courage,

---

[108] Like Aesara, Perictione is not listed among the Pythagoreans in the *Catalogue*. Rather, our sources introduce Perictione as the Athenian mother of Plato and a descendant of Solon (D.L. 3.1–2). The suggestion is twofold: first, Perictione's Athenian lineage might be the reason why, unlike the other Doric pseudepigrapha, *On Harmony* is written in Ionic dialect with only occasional Dorisms. Second, and most important, Perictione would be an effective pseudonym, for it strategically bridges the gap between Platonism and Pythagoreanism by creating a strong biological connection between Plato and his allegedly Pythagorean mother.

[109] Stobaeus quotes Fr. 2 first, in the section of the *Eclogues* concerning parents and children, and Fr. 1 later, in the section about the household. However, the ring composition of Fr. 1 (see the next footnote) and the initial more general ethical statement prompts the assumption that this functioned as the introduction of the treatise.

[110] This initial ethical statement is repeated almost *verbatim* at the end of Fr. 1, where again the harmonious woman is described as 'full of intelligence and moderation' (Thesleff 144.23–145.6). In this instance, however, harmony is only said to benefit a woman's husband, relatives, friends, and the members of her household. Hence, in the conclusion of the fragment, the parallelism with the woman's own soul and the wider city is lost.

moderation, and justice. Second, this betters at once the individual, private, and public spheres.

The relation with Aesara is threefold. First, Aesara lists the parts of the soul without specifying their virtues but only making general claims about the virtue of justice being the orderly arrangement of these parts. On the other hand, Perictione lists the virtues but does not link this to the tripartition of the soul into mind, spirit, and desire. The connection between these two psychological and ethical theories is made explicit in other Doric treatises, such as Metopos' *On Virtue* (Stob. 3.1.115; Thesleff 118.7–13) and Theages' *On Virtue* (Stob. 3.1.117; Thesleff 190.19–25). Second, whilst in *On Human Nature* the emphasis is placed on justice, which is the virtue of each part of the soul performing its function, in *On Harmony* the primary virtue is intelligence, which is listed as the first virtue of the harmonious woman, alongside the traditional female virtue of moderation. According to Centrone, the same tension between the leading role of justice and *phronēsis* is found in other Doric treatises and can be traced back to Plato himself (2014: 330).[111] Finally, like Aesara, Perictione describes harmony as beneficial to both households and cities. Yet, whilst Aesara writes about the human nature, or soul, in general, Perictione specifically applies this argument to womankind.

Unlike Aesara the metaphysician and cosmologist, then, the author of *On Harmony* presents herself as a female philosopher writing about female moral-ity. Another Doric treatise ascribed to a Pythagorean woman and discussing what virtue is, which virtues are especially female, and what makes women truly excellent is *On the Moderation of Women*, written under the name of the Pythagorean woman Phintys of Sparta, daughter of Callicrates.[112] Perictione echoes Aesara and describes as harmonious the woman who is fully virtuous:

---

[111] In *On Intelligence and Good Fortune*, Damippos makes *phronēsis* responsible for the good order of the soul (Fr. 1, Stob. 3.3.63; Thesleff 68.4–18) and describes it as the mother of virtues (Fr. 2, in Stob. 3.3.64; Thesleff 69.14–5). In *On Justice*, Ekkelos calls *dikaiosynē* 'mother' (Stob. 3.9.51; Thesleff 78.1).

[112] The *Catalogue of the Pythagoreans* lists a woman named Philtys, whose father is named Theocris and comes from Croton. Since Stobaeus introduces Phintys as a Spartan and the daughter of Callicrates, it is unclear whether this is meant to be the same philosopher. A similar name, Callicras, is attached to the Pythagorean pseudepigraphic treatise *On the Happiness of the Household* (Frs. 1–2, in Stob. 4.22.101, 28.16–8; Thesleff 103.1–107.11). This in turn may refer to Callicratides, whom Diogenes introduces as the brother of Empedocles (8.53). On Empedocles' connection with Pythagoreanism, see also D.L. 8.54–56 (on the evidence of Timaeus, Neanthes (Fr. 26), Hermippus, and the rhetorician Alcidamas), in which he is described as one of Pythagoras' pupils, banned from the school together with Philolaus for publishing Pythagoras' secret teachings. According to Eusebius, Empedocles was the disciple of Pythagoras' son and successor Telauges (*PE* 10.14.15 – see also D.L. 8.42), and, according to a spurious letter from Telauges to Philolaus (D.L. 8.55), he studied with the Pythagoreans Brontinus and Hippasus, who was later also exiled for breaking the vow of silence (Iamblichus, *On the General Science of Mathematics* 25).

the good woman should be in possession of all forms of excellence, including *phronēsis*, intelligence. By contrast, in *On Moderation*, Phintys gives a different definition of virtue, which is less focused on *phronēsis* and, as the title suggests, more on *sōphrosynē*, moderation. At first reading, then, Phintys appears to paint a conflicting, and more traditional, picture of the excellent woman.

Like *On Harmony*, *On Moderation* also revolves around the question of the good woman. The author named Phintys the Spartan writes that to be good, women should be virtuous. She then raises the question of which virtues are appropriate for women and, as a result of this, whether women should dedicate themselves to a life of wisdom and practise philosophy. Again, the treatise can be divided into two parts. In the introduction, Phintys proposes an original ethical theory about what virtue is and which virtues are most suitably female (Stob. 4.23.61; Thesleff 151.20–152.18). The answer is that the virtue that belongs to women above all is *sōphrosynē*, moderation. Yet this should not preclude them from philosophising. Next, Phintys moves on to a series of case studies of how women can prove themselves to be excellent in everyday life (Stob. 4.23.61-1a, Thesleff 152.18–154.11). Specifically, she identifies five areas in which a woman shows moderation: the relationship with her husband, decency in clothing, the relationship with the other members of her household, avoidance of mystery rites, and religious sacrifices (Thesleff 152.19–24). The argument in the first part of the treatise is the following.

> A woman must be completely good and well-behaved, for without virtue she would never become so. For the virtue of each thing makes that which is receptive of it excellent. The virtue of the eyes makes the eyes excellent, that of the ears the ears, and that of a horse horses. Finally, the virtue of a man makes men excellent. And similarly, the virtue of a woman makes women excellent. The virtue that above all belongs to women is moderation, for through this virtue they will be able to honour and love their spouses. Yet many may think that it is not fitting for a woman to philosophise, just as it is not fitting for her to ride a horse and speak in public. *But I think* that some things are proper to men, others to women, others are common to men and women, and again some of these belong more to men than women and others more to women than men. Proper to men is fighting, political activity, and public speaking. Proper to women is staying at home and indoors, welcoming and serving the husband. *And I say* that courage, justice, and intelligence are common. For just as the virtues of the body are suited to both women and men, so too the virtues of the soul. The virtues of the body are health, strength, good perception, and beauty. Some of these are more appropriate for men to exercise and possess, others for women. For courage and intelligence are more for men because of both the constitution of their bodies and the capacity of their souls, but moderation is for women.
>
> (Stob. 4.23.61; Thesleff 151.20–152.18, emphasis added)

The introduction of *On Moderation* is in turn divided into two parts:[113] first, the author offers a general definition of what virtue is and uses this to show that the proper female virtue is moderation (Thesleff 151.20–152.5). Second, the author discusses whether virtues are the same for men and women, and thus elaborates on the previous claim and the extent to which moderation is most suitably female (152.5–18). Noteworthy is that the latter is introduced as an *ad hominem* argument whose critical targets are those who think that women are not suited for philosophy. As I show below, Phintys writes that men and women have the same virtues in order to argue for women's ability to philosophise. Therefore, the focus of the treatise is on moderation as a female virtue, but in passing, this leads Phintys to discuss the extent to which philosophy can be a female activity. Phintys aims to show how women can be virtuous and display moderation in their daily life without turning a blind eye to their philosophical skills.

The argument in the first section can be unpacked as follows: a general definition of virtue (151.21–152.1), an argument by analogy (152.1–4), and the application of this general theory to the case of women (151.4–5). First, Phintys writes that virtue (*aretē*) makes us excellent (*spoudaios*). The reason for this lies in the so-called functionalist theory of virtue,[114] according to which *aretē* is what makes one perform one's function, or job, at best. In the *Republic*, Plato introduces the notion of function (*ergon*) as that which either one alone can do or one does better than anyone or anything else: for example, the function of a horse is what horses do better than any other animals, and the function of the eyes is seeing because one cannot do so with any other sense organ (1.352d-e). In turn, virtue is that which enables one to perform the *ergon* well (1.353b). Therefore, if eyes are the sense organ for sight, virtuous or excellent eyes can see better than other eyes.[115] Plato thus describes virtue as *oikeia*, appropriate, belonging to a thing's nature and pertaining to its role (1.353e).[116] For Plato, then, virtue is a form of excellence at performing one's proper function. Similarly, according to Phintys, a virtuous human, animal, or thing excels at being a human, animal, or thing.

---

[113] For a more detailed analysis of the fragments and the comparison with Plato and Aristotle's theories of virtue, see Pellò (2020b).

[114] A similar theory is also proposed by Aristotle in the *Nicomachean Ethics* (1.7.11.1097b31-15.1098a17). For an overview of the functionalist argument for virtue, with special focus on Aristotle, see Barney (2008).

[115] In the *Nicomachean Ethics*, Aristotle also argues that the difference between a harper and an excellent harper is that the latter does not simply play the harp, but rather performs this activity well: she achieves goodness as a harper. Similarly, a human and an excellent human perform the same function, namely living in accordance with reason, but the latter performs this uniquely human activity well (1.7.14–15.1098a7-17).

[116] See also *Meno* 72a, where virtue is determined 'for each one of us in relation to each function (*ergon*) and according to each activity and age'.

In the next section of the argument, this general definition is applied to the same examples Plato uses in the *Republic*. Specifically, that a good woman is an excellent woman is supported inductively with three analogies: just as virtuous eyes, virtuous horses, and virtuous men are excellent eyes, horses, and men, so are virtuous women excellent women. Finally, Phintys employs the *ergon* argument to find which virtue belongs to women most of all: since virtue is that which enables an agent to perform her job at best, since Phintys describes a woman's job as honouring and loving her husband, and since the virtue which enables women to do so well is moderation, the preliminary conclusion is that moderation (*sōphrosynē*) is mostly female. Specifically, Phintys writes that moderation is the most appropriate (*oikeia*) virtue for women to exercise and possess.

This first argument is in line with the title of the treatise, *On Moderation*, and the second part of the fragment, in which Phintys shows how women act with moderation towards their family members and their household (Stob. 4.23.61-1a, Thesleff 152.18–154.11). Yet this seems in contrast with Perictione's argument in *On Harmony* that women should be full of all virtues. Furthermore, so far Phintys' version of the *ergon* argument mirrors the one by Plato in the *Republic*. Like Plato, Phintys states that each thing has an appropriate (*oikeia*) excellence, or virtue (*aretē*), and that being virtuous means being excellent (*spoudaios*) at one's job. Moreover, like Plato, Phintys uses inductive arguments, or arguments by analogy, according to which the links to the excellence of animals, such as horses, and parts of the body, such as the eyes and ears, enable us to infer what the excellence of a human and specifically a woman is. These overlapping similarities may lead one to wonder whether there is any original idea Phintys contributes to ancient virtue ethics and, if so, what this contribution is. Nonetheless, in the next section of the argument, Phintys explicitly distinguishes her view of women's activities and virtues from that of the majority, thus suggesting that her theory is somewhat novel. As we shall see, this also brings Phintys closer to Perictione in arguing that women have *phronēsis*, intelligence.

After concluding that moderation is a female virtue, Phintys turns to those who believe that women are not suited for philosophy, just as they are not suited for riding and public speaking. Worthy of attention, especially given the possibility that this treatise may in fact have been authored by a woman, is that Phintys writes in the first person with clearly polemical tones ('But I think . . . '). At first reading, and similar to Aesara's *On Human Nature*, her reply seems based on a tripartition of things. Specifically, Phintys distinguishes those things that are proper (*idia*)[117] and thus belong either only to men or only to women, those that are common

---

[117] Aristotle, too, describes functions as *idia*, proper (*NE* 1.7.12.1097b34).

(*koina*) to both men and women, and those that belong more (*mallon*) to men or more to women. In the first category, she places activities such as fighting, politics, and public speaking for men, and domestic life for women. In the second category, she lists both the virtues, or excellences, of the body, such as health, beauty, sense-perception, and strength, and the virtues of the soul, namely justice, courage, and intelligence.[118] Third, she divides the common virtues further into two subcategories: those that are more for men and those that are more for women. This shows that what initially appeared as a simple tripartite structure is in fact a more complex categorisation of things into classes and subclasses. For example, courage is listed both as common to men and women and as preferably male. The virtues that are preferable for men are intelligence (*phronēsis*) and courage (*andreia*), whereas the one that is more for women is moderation (*sōphrosynē*). The reason for this, Phintys writes, is twofold: the different constitutions of their bodies[119] and capacities of their souls.[120] Thus, in response to the many, Phintys does not reject that in some respect, men and women are different and that such differences impact on their activities and virtues. Yet, as we shall see, this is not used as an argument to deny that women can philosophise.

Two problems remain open: what impact does the second section of the argument have on the claim in the first section that moderation is the virtue that is most appropriate for women? And how exactly does this tripartition help Phintys respond to those who think that women should not philosophise? In the first part of the argument, Phintys reaches the conclusion that moderation is the virtue that most of all (*malista*) belongs to women, for it enables them to perform their domestic function at best. The second part refines this statement: moderation is not exclusively female, but rather it is preferably female. Moderation is not listed among those things that are proper to the female gender, like domestic life. Rather, Phintys writes that this virtue simply belongs more (*mallon*) to women than men. In the light of the first part of the argument, one may claim that moderation belongs mostly (*malista*) to women. This leaves open the possibility that men too should act with moderation. Similarly, intelligence and courage are first listed among those things that are common to both sexes and then as examples of virtues that are preferably male, which suggests

---

[118] Similarly, in *Meno* 71a-73a Socrates separates himself from the many, who ascribe one kind of excellence to men and a completely different one to women, and notices that, just as there is no such thing as a different kind of health or strength for men and women, male and female virtues are the same. Once again, Plato and Phintys use the same examples – namely, bodily features – to reach similar conclusions – namely, that virtues are common to both sexes.

[119] In *Republic* 5.451d-455e, Plato also writes that men and women have different bodies and physical strengths but does not use this to argue for differences in virtue.

[120] The reference might be to Aristotle's claim that men and women have different psychological faculties and that, specifically, the female rational capacity is 'without authority' (*Politics* 1.13.1259b38-1260a7).

that both men and women are intelligent and courageous, but it is preferable for men to be so. A more challenging issue is why Phintys proposes the tripartition and whether she is successful in discrediting the opinion of the many and showing that women can philosophise. The many believe that activities like philosophising, riding, and public speaking are not for women. Phintys agrees that public speaking is proper to men and not for women but does not list philosophy as an example of uniquely male activity. In contrast, she distinguishes public speaking, which is exclusively male, from virtues like intelligence and courage, which are shared by men and women alike, but nonetheless are preferably male. The suggestion seems to be that, like virtues, some activities, too, are common to both sexes. For example, like intelligence, philosophy may be common, despite perhaps being more for men.

Overall, Phintys uses similar arguments, language, and examples as her philosophical predecessors but nevertheless adds a novel twist to their ethical theories by introducing the notion of preferable virtue. *On Moderation*, then, is a further example of how the Pythagorean pseudepigrapha depict women as philosophers. Specifically, like Perictione in *On Harmony*, Phintys is a female ethicist and an expert on female morality and virtues. The last Doric treatise, *On Wisdom*, which is also ascribed to Perictione, builds the picture of the Pythagorean woman as an epistemologist and metaphysician.

3.2.3 Perictione on What Philosophy is All About

The last item on the list of Doric treatises ascribed to women philosophers in the pseudepigrapha is *On Wisdom*.[121] Like *On Harmony*, this text is written under the name of Plato's mother, Perictione. Yet it draws a rather different image of the Pythagorean woman philosopher: rather than an expert on female morality, Perictione is an authority in metaphysics and epistemology.

On Wisdom is a theoretical treatise that revolves around the question of what wisdom is and why one should embark on philosophical activities. In the two available fragments, Perictione makes two claims: first, humans aim at contemplation of all things. Second, wisdom is the highest-ranked human activity, for its function is to grasp all kinds of things and bring humans closer to the divine. This is supported with the introduction of a tripartition of sciences, where

---

[121] The source is Stobaeus. This treatise shows substantial textual overlap with another pseudepigraphic text, also titled *On Wisdom*, but attributed to the 4th-century Pythagorean Archytas of Tarentum and preserved in Iamblichus' *Protrepticus* (Thesleff 43.25–45.4). This led Huffman (2005: 591–8) and Horky (2015: 33–6) to question the attribution to Perictione in Stobaeus. The relationship between these two versions of *On Wisdom* is discussed in detail by Giulia De Cesaris (De Cesaris and Pellò, forthcoming). For the purpose of this Element, suffice it to notice that in Stobaeus *On Wisdom* becomes associated with a woman philosopher.

human wisdom is ranked higher than any other theoretical activity. Again, tripartite divisions and functionalist accounts are recurring argumentative devices in the pseudepigrapha.

> The human was born and is constituted for the purpose of contemplating the reason of the nature of the universe; and the function of wisdom is to obtain this very thing and to contemplate the intelligence of the things-that-are. Thus, geometry, too, as well as arithmetic and the other theoretical activities (also called sciences), engage with the things that are, but wisdom engages with all the kinds of things that are. For wisdom relates to all things that are, just as sight relates to all things that are visible and hearing to all things that are hearable. Moreover, among the attributes pertaining to the things that are, some pertain universally to all, some to most of them, and others in some way to each individual thing. Thus, to behold and contemplate what pertains universally to all things, belongs to wisdom, whereas it belongs to natural science to contemplate what pertains to most things, and to the science of something determinate to contemplate the peculiar attributes of each thing. And therefore, wisdom retrieves the principles of the things that are altogether, whereas physics retrieves the principles of what comes to be by nature, and geometry, arithmetic, and music the principles concerning quantity and the harmonious. Hence, whoever is able to resolve all kinds to one and the same principle and from this compose and enumerate them again, this person seems to be both wisest and truest. Moreover, this person has found a good lookout point, from which one will be able to behold the god as well as all things that have been placed in his column and order.
>
>   (Frs. 1–2, in Stob. 3.1.120–1; Thesleff 146.2–22)[122]

On Wisdom can be divided into three sections: an introductory statement concerning the purpose of human beings and the function of wisdom (Fr. 1, in Stob 3.1.120; Thesleff 146.2–5); a comparison between wisdom and the other quantitative and qualitative sciences (Fr. 2, in Stob. 3.1.121; Thesleff 146.6–14); and a conclusive statement on the importance of attaining wisdom (Fr. 2, in Stob. 3.1.121; Thesleff 146.6–14). First, Perictione writes that humans are made for contemplating the reason (*logos*) of all of nature. She complements this with an *ergon* argument, according to which the function of wisdom is to obtain such *logos* and contemplate all that is. Like Aesara and Phintys, Perictione defines things based on what they do, their function, or *ergon*. Like Aesara, Perictione places humans in a privileged position in virtue of their ability to inspect the world around them.

Next, Perictione elaborates on what it means for wisdom to be set over what is. She first distinguishes wisdom from other sciences with the help of an

---

[122] This translation is adapted from a forthcoming article on Perictione I co-wrote with De Cesaris. The article also includes a thorough analysis of the argument, the discussion of the original Greek, and a detailed comparison with Aristotle's metaphysics.

argument by analogy between wisdom and the bodily senses and then organises the sciences and their objects into three categories. The argument opens with a list of disciplines, such as geometry, arithmetic, and other sciences, which all focus on the things that are. Wisdom, too, is set upon the things that are, but differently from other sciences, it focuses on 'all the kinds of things that are.' This is supported by comparing wisdom to sight and hearing: just as sight is set upon everything visible and hearing is set upon everything hearable, the object of wisdom is everything that exists. Similar analogies with sense organs are found in Aesara's *On Human Nature* and Phintys' *On Moderation*.

Perictione further characterises wisdom by means of two tripartitions: an ontological tripartition of things and an epistemological tripartition of sciences. First, she distinguishes three groups of objects: those which pertain to all things, those which pertain to most things, and those which pertain to each thing in a particular way. Next, she distinguishes three sciences and maps this epistemological tripartition onto the tripartition of objects from the previous lines: wisdom contemplates what pertains to all things universally, natural sciences contemplate what pertains to most things, the science concerning something determinate contemplates particular features which pertain to each thing. In the last lines, the tripartition is revised: wisdom is said to investigate the principles of the things that are, physics those of what comes to be in accordance with nature, and the third group of sciences the principles of particular classes of beings, such as those having a magnitude in the case of mathematics and the harmonious in the case of music. This passage recalls Aristotle's own division of the different branches of learning in the *Metaphysics* (6.1.1025b3-1026a32). Aristotle organises theoretical sciences into three groups: first, philosophy, natural sciences, and mathematics. The difference is that Perictione calls the highest form of learning wisdom (*sophia*).

In the conclusion, wisdom is said to be what enables humans to contemplate the divine. Like Aesara, Perictione ranks humans higher than any other being in virtue of their ability to contemplate. This is the reason why scholars interpret *On Wisdom* as protreptic (Horky, 2015). This treatise urges humans towards contemplation and encourages the audience, which arguably includes women as well as men, to live a life of wisdom and engage in philosophical activity.

Overall, what should be noted is that, like Aesara's *On Nature*, Perictione's treatise is not explicitly gendered: the author writes about humans in general, not women specifically and exclusively. In *On Wisdom*, Perictione is presented as the sage mastering all sciences and living a philosophical way of life – that is, the best and highest form of life. Perictione is presented as a philosopher not insofar as she writes about women but to the extent that she knows about the nature of things.

3.3 Further Conclusions

Another issue raised by Marguerite Deslauriers is that the Pythagorean women pseudepigraphers are credited with writing about feminine topics such as home economics, married life, and female virtues, which in antiquity were not considered strictly philosophical (2012: 244). Thus, our challenge has been to show that the Pythagorean women's pseudepigrapha are philosophically valuable. My suggestion is that these four treatises are philosophical in two ways, by portraying the Pythagorean women as both female ethicists and metaphysicians.

From the Hellenistic period onwards, the Pythagorean women are credited with writing two sorts of texts: letters to younger female pupils teaching them how to behave with their husbands, children, and household; and treatises about either virtue or, to a lesser extent, the workings of the cosmos. While the letters include personal messages about women's daily activities, the treatises comprise fully fledged philosophical arguments. The ethical treatises tackle the question of what virtue is, to which Phintys answers that virtue is what makes one excellent at doing one's job, as well as the question of how the virtues are related and what it means to be full of virtue, to which Perictione answers that this makes one harmonious. After these general statements, both Perictione and Phintys turn to the female gender and discuss how women can be virtuous. They both agree that women should have *sōphrosynē*, moderation. Perictione also argues that women should be full of *phronēsis*, intelligence, courage, and justice. Phintys, on the other hand, acknowledges that virtues are common to both men and women and therefore women, too, can have intelligence alongside moderation. As such, *On Harmony* and *On Moderation* raise general philosophical questions, which they then apply to the particular case of women's domestic life. They start from vexed philosophical issues, such as the definition of virtue as excellence and the relationship between the virtues of the body and the virtues of the soul, and then move on to discussing how women, too, can partake in this more general ancient theory of virtue. Thus, Perictione and Phintys draw the picture of the Pythagorean female sage as an expert of ethics and someone who has knowledge of women's morality and virtues.

The theoretical treatises, on the other hand, raise different concerns that are not evidently and exclusively connected to the female gender, family life, and the domestic sphere. The first question is what makes the cosmos, the city, the household, and the soul a harmonious system, to which Aesara replies that each system should have its many different parts arranged in order with the superior part, such as the mind, having a greater share of power. This leads Aesara to discuss the structure of the soul, the leading role of *nous*, and the superiority of human beings who have within themselves the ordering principle of justice and concord that applies to both the city and the family. Perictione also takes humans to be the closest to the divine in virtue of their ability to contemplate the cosmos and everything in it. Human wisdom is said to be the highest human theoretical activity. Thus, the authors of *On Human Nature* and *On Wisdom* are experts on the structure of the cosmos, knowledge, and the soul.

Overall, like our sources for ancient Pythagoreanism, the Hellenistic and post-Hellenistic texts, too, portray the Pythagorean woman as a two-faced sage, who philosophises about a wide variety of topics, which include but are not restricted to the female sphere. Something for future researchers to explore is whether, and if so how, the pseudepigraphic letters contribute to this picture.

4 Final Remarks: Gendered Knowledge and Genderless Wisdom

Dutsch writes that the Pythagorean women are viewed as philosophers 'whose ability does not differ from men' (2020: 214). The Element has looked at the Pythagorean women and their various contributions to the Pythagorean tradition in two steps: firstly, I analysed the available evidence for women in 5th-century Pythagorean communities and, secondly, I unpacked the arguments in the pseudepigraphic treatises ascribed to Pythagorean female authors.

The evidence for women in ancient Pythagoreanism is four-fold: first, women are said to be part of Pythagoras' larger audiences and attend his public lectures; second, women are also included in the list of Pythagoras' select disciples; third, some women are recorded as members of Pythagoras' family, such as his wife Theano, who distinguish themselves in virtue of their domestic roles within the family; finally, we know of at least one woman, Timycha, who was known for practising the Pythagorean way of life. I also noted that in the Hellenistic period, we come across precepts and sayings attributed to Theano, which primarily focus on marriage but also include references to the doctrine of the afterlife and the cosmological role of numbers.

Whether the early Pythagorean women advanced philosophical arguments of their own is unknown. Nonetheless, in the Hellenistic and Imperial Age, these women became the alleged authors of letters and treatises, which include original philosophical theories and ideas. Regardless of who first produced the pseudepigrapha, they were handed down to us under the names of women philosophers, such as Theano and Perictione. The letters are about women reacting to their unfaithful husbands and raising their children in luxury. The ethical treatises focus on virtues and discuss the relation between justice, courage, intelligence, and self-restraint. The theoretical treatises, whose authorship is more frequently called into question, are about numbers as the ultimate principles of all things, the world order, and the value of philosophy. My conclusion is that these arguments are all considered appropriate for a woman philosopher.

Overall, the knowledge and expertise our sources attribute to the Pythagorean female sage are primarily gendered, women-centred, but at times become genderless, universal. Whether this be a matter of living philosophically or writing about philosophical topics, the Pythagorean women are considered capable of doing philosophy.

Abbreviations

Ar. *Met.*	Aristotle, *Metaphysics*
Ar. *NE*	Aristotle, *Nicomachean Ethics*
Ath.	Athenaeus, *Deipnosophistae*
Clem. *Strom.*	Clement, *Stromata*
D.L.	Diogenes Laertius, *Lives of Eminent Philosophers*
DK	Diels, H., and Kranz, W. (1951–1952) (eds.). *Die Fragmente der Vorsokratiker*, Berlin: Weidmann
Eus. *PE*	Eusebius, *Praeparatio Evangelica*
FGrHist	Jacoby, F. (1995). *Die Fragmente der Griechischen Historiker*, Leiden: Brill
Hdt.	Herodotus, *Histories*
Iamb. *VP*	Iamblichus, *Vita Pythagorica*
Onom.	Julius Pollux, *Onomasticon*
Pl. *Rep.*	Plato, *Republic*
Porph. *VP*	Porphyry, *Life of Pythagoras*
Stob. *Ecl.*	Stobaues *Eclogues*
Stob. *Flor.*	Stobaeus, *Florilegium*

Glossary of Names

Early Pythagoreanism

Arignote	Pythagoras' daughter
Babelyca	Pythagoras' follower, listed in the *Catalogue of the Pythagoreans*
Bitale	Damo's daughter, Pythagoras' granddaughter
Boeo	Pythagoras' follower, listed in the *Catalogue*
Cheilonis	Pythagoras' follower, listed in the *Catalogue*
Cleaichma	Pythagoras' follower, listed in the *Catalogue*
Cratesicleia	Pythagoras' follower, listed in the *Catalogue*
Damo	Pythagoras' daughter
Deino	Pythagoras' follower, wife of Brotinus
Eccelo	Pythagoras' follower, listed in the *Catalogue*
Echecrateia	Pythagoras' follower, listed in the *Catalogue*
Habroteleia	Pythagoras' follower, listed in the *Catalogue*
Lastheneia	Pythagoras' follower, listed in the *Catalogue*
Myia	Pythagoras' daughter
Occelo	Pythagoras' follower, listed in the *Catalogue*
Peisirrhode	Pythagoras' follower, listed in the *Catalogue*
Philtys	Pythagoras' follower, listed in the *Catalogue*
Pythais	Pythagoras' mother
Sara	Pythagoras' daughter
Theadusa	Pythagoras' follower, listed in the *Catalogue*
Theano	Pythagoras' wife and best-known disciple
Themistoclea	Pythagoras' alleged sister and teacher
Timycha	Pythagoras' follower, wife of Myllias
Tyrsenis	Pythagoras' follower, listed in the *Catalogue*

Pseudepigrapha

Aesara	Author of *On Human Nature*
Melissa	Author of the letter to Cleareta
Myia	Author of the letter to Phillys
Perictione	Author of *On the Harmony of Women* and *On Wisdom*
Phintys	Author of *On the Moderation of Women*
Theano	Author of *On Piety* and the letters to Callisto, Eubule, Euclides, Eurydice, Nicostrate, Timareta, Timonides, and Rhodope

References

Allen, P. (1985). *The Concept of Woman: The Aristotelian Revolution, 750 BC–AD 1250*. Grand Rapids: M. B. Eerdmans.

Bagnall, R. S., and Cribiore, R. (2006). *Women's Letters from Ancient Egypt, 300 BC–AD 800*. Ann Arbor: University of Michigan Press.

Barker, A. (2014). Pythagorean Harmonics. In Huffman 2014a, pp. 185–203.

Barney, R. (2008). Aristotle's Argument for a Human Function. *Oxford Studies in Ancient Philosophy*, 34, 293–332.

Betegh, G. (2014). Pythagoreans, Orphism and Greek Religion. In Huffman 2014a, pp. 149–66.

Brodersen, K. (2014). *Pythagorean Women: Their History and Writings*. Bryn Mawr Classical Review. https://bmcr.brynmawr.edu/2014/2014.08.58/

Burkert, W. (1982). Craft versus Sect: The Problem of Orphics and Pythagoreans. In B. F. Meyers and E. P. Sanders, eds., *Jewish and Christian Self-Definition*. Philadelphia: SCM Press, pp. 14–19.

Burkert, W. (1972). *Lore and Science in Ancient Pythagoreanism*. Cambridge, MA: Cambridge University Press.

Burkert, W. (1960), Platon oder Pythagoras? Zum Ursprung des Wortes 'Philosophie'. *Hermes* 88(2), 159–77.

Caizzi, F. D. (1966). *Antisthenes: Fragmenta*. Milano: Istituto Editoriale Cisaplino.

Centrone, B. (2014). The Pseudo-Pythagorean Writings. In Huffman 2014a, pp. 315–40.

Centrone, B. (1996). *Introduzione ai Pitagorici*. Roma: Laterza.

Centrone, B. (1990). *Pseudopitagorica Ethica*. Napoli: Bibliopolis.

Cornelli, G. (2013). *In Search of Pythagoreanism*. Berlin: De Gruyter.

De Cesaris, G., and Pellò, C. (forthcoming). Perictione, Mother of Metaphysics: A New Philosophical Reading of *On Wisdom*. In K. R. O'Reilly and C. Pellò, eds., *Ancient Women Philosophers*. Cambridge: Cambridge University Press.

Demand, N. H. (1982). The Position of Women in Pythagoreanism. In *Thebes in the Fifth Century: Heracles Resurgent*. London: Routledge, pp. 132–5.

Demand, N. H. (1973). Pythagoras, Son of Mnesarchos. *Phronesis*, 18(2), 91–6.

Deslauriers, M. (2012). Women, Education, and Philosophy. In S. L. James and S. Dillon, eds., *A Companion to Women in the Ancient World*. Chichester: Wiley-Blackwell, pp. 343–53.

Diels, H., and Kranz, W. (eds.) (1951–1952). *Die Fragmente der Vorsokratiker*. Berlin: Weidmann.

Dillon, J. (2014). Pythagoreanism in the Academic Tradition: The Early Academy to Numenius. In Huffman 2014a, pp. 250–73.

Dillon, J., and Hershbell, J. (1991). *Iamblichus: On the Pythagorean Way of Life*. Atlanta: Scholars Press.

Dorandi, T. (1989). Assiotea e Lastenia: Due Donne all'Accademia. *Atti e Memorie Accademia Toscana 'La Colombaria'*, 54, 53–66.

Dutsch, D. (2020). *Pythagorean Women Philosophers: Between Belief and Suspicion*. Oxford: Oxford University Press.

Flinterman, J. J. (2014). Pythagoreans in Rome and Asia Minor around the Turn of the Common Era. In Huffman 2014a, pp. 341–59.

Fortenbaugh, W. W. (2007). Biography and the Aristotelian Peripatos. In M. Erler and S. Schorn, eds., *Die Griechische Biographie in Hellenistischer Zeit*. Berlin: De Gruyter, pp. 45–78.

Fortenbaugh, W. W., and Schtrumpf, E. (2017). *Dicaearchus of Messana*. Abingdon: Routledge.

von Fritz, K. (1940). *Pythagorean Politics in Southern Italy: An Analysis of the Sources*. New York: Columbia University Press.

Gemelli Marciano, L. (2014), The Pythagorean Way of Life and Pythagorean Ethics. In C. A. Huffman, ed., *A History of Pythagoreanism*. Cambridge University Press, pp. 131–48.

Graziosi, B. (2013). *Pythagorean Women: Their History and Writings* by Sarah B. Pomeroy. www.timeshighereducation.com/books/pythagorean-women-their-history-and-writings-by-sarah-b-pomeroy/2009266.article#survey-answer

Hadot, P. (1995), *Philosophy as a Way of Life: Spiritual Exercises from Socrates to Foucault*. Oxford: Blackwell.

Hadot, P. (2002), *What Is Ancient Philosophy?* Cambridge, MA: Harvard University Press.

Haskins, E. (2005). Pythagorean Women. In M. Ballif and M. G. Moran, eds., *Classical Rhetorics and Rhetoricians*. Westport: Praeger, pp. 315–19.

Hawley, R. (1994). The Problem of Women Philosophers in Ancient Greece. In L. J. Archer, S. Fischler, and M. Wyke, eds., *Women in Ancient Societies*. Hong Kong: Macmillan, pp. 70–87.

Hercher, R. (1873), *Epistolographi Graeci*. Paris: A.F. Didot.

Hercher, R. (ed.) (1965). *Epistolographi Graeci*. Amsterdam: A. M. Hakkert.

Horky, P. S. (2015). Pseudo-Archytas' Protreptics? On Wisdom in its Contexts. In D. Nails and H. Tarrant, eds., *Second Sailing: Alternative Perspectives on Plato*. Helsinki: Societas Scientiarum Fennica, pp. 21–40.

Horky, P. S. (2013). *Plato and Pythagoreanism*. Oxford: Oxford University Press.

Huffman, C. A. (2019). Pythagoreanism. In E. Zalta, ed., *The Stanford Encyclopaedia of Philosophy.* https://plato.stanford.edu/archives/win2016/entries/pythagoreanism/

Huffman, C. A. (2018). Pythagoras. In E. Zalta, ed., *The Stanford Encyclopaedia of Philosophy.* https://plato.stanford.edu/archives/sum2014/entries/pythagoras/

Huffman, C. A. (ed.) (2014a). *A History of Pythagoreanism.* Cambridge: Cambridge University Press.

Huffman, C. A. (2014b). The Peripatetics on the Pythagoreans. In *Huffman* 2014a, pp. 274–95.

Huffman, C. A. (2012). *Aristoxenus of Tarentum.* New Brunswick: Transaction.

Huffman, C. A. (2008a). The 'Pythagorean Precepts' of Aristoxenus: Crucial Evidence for Pythagorean Moral Philosophy. *The Classical Quarterly,* 58, 104–19.

Huffman, C. A. (2008b). Two Problems in Pythagoreanism. In P. Curd and D. W. Graham, eds., *The Oxford Handbook of Presocratic Philosophy.* Oxford: Oxford University Press, pp. 284–301.

Huffman, C. A. (2005). *Archytas of Tarentum.* Cambridge: Cambridge University Press.

Huizenga, A. B. (2013). *Moral Education for Women in the Pastoral and Pythagorean Letters.* Boston: Brill.

Izzi, F. (2009). *Viaggio nell' universo femminile della Magna Grecia.* Vicenza: Altromondo.

Jacoby, F. (1995). *Die Fragmente der Griechischen Historiker.* Leiden: Brill.

Kingsley, P. (1995). *Ancient Philosophy, Mystery, and Magic: Empedocles and the Pythagorean Tradition.* Oxford: Oxford University Press.

Kirk, G. S., Raven, J. E., and Schofield, M. (1983), *The Presocratic Philosophers.* Cambridge University Press.

Laks, A. (2014). Diogenes Laertius' *Life of Pythagoras.* In Huffman 2014a, pp. 360–80.

Lambropoulou, V. (1995). Some Pythagorean Female Virtues. In R. Hawley and B. Levick, eds., *Women in Antiquity: New Assessments.* London: Routledge, pp. 122–34.

Lefkowitz, M. R., and Fant, M. B. (2005). *Women's Life in Greece and Rome.* London: Duckworth.

Lloyd, G. E. R. (2014). Pythagoras. In Huffman 2014a, pp. 24–45.

Macris, C. (2016). Aisara, Perictione, Phintys, Ptolemais, Rhodope, Theano. In R. Goulet, ed., *Dictionnaire des Philosophes Antiques.* Paris: CNRS Editions.

Macris, C. (2014). Porphyry's *Life of Pythagoras.* In Huffman 2014a, pp. 381–98.

Macris, C. (2013), Carismatic Authority, Spirirtual Guide, and Way of Life in the Pythagorean Tradition. In M. Chase, S. L. R. Clarke, M. McGhee, eds., *Philosophy as a Way of Life: Ancients and Modern. Essays in Honour of Pierre Hadot.* Chichester: Wiley-Blackwell, pp. 57–83.

Ménage, G. (1984). *The History of Women Philosophers.* Lanham: University Press of America.

Meunier, M. (1932). *Femmes Pythagoriciennes.* Paris: L'Artisan du Livre.

Migliorati, M. (2020). Le donne della scuola pitagorica: L'analisi dell'anima in uno scritto di Esara di Lucania. In M. Bonelli, ed., *Filosofe, Maestre, e Imperatrici.* Roma: Edizioni di Storia e Letteratura, pp. 79–104.

Minar, E. L. (1942). *Early Pythagorean Politics in Practice and Theory.* Baltimore: Waverly Press.

Montepaone, C. (ed.) (2011). *Pitagoriche: Scritti Femminili di Età Ellenistica.* Bari: EdiPuglia.

Montepaone, C. (1993). Theano la Pitagorica. In S. Georgoudi and N. Loraux, eds., *La Grecia al Femminile.* Roma: Laterza, pp. 73–105.

Montepaone, C., and Catarzi, M. (2016), Pythagorean Askesis in Timycha of Sparta and Theano of Croton. In A.-B. Renger and A. Stavru, eds., *Pythagorean Knowledge from the Ancient to the Modern World.* Wiesbaden: Harrasowitz Verlag, pp. 135–50.

Nails, D. (1989). The Pythagorean Women Philosophers: Ethics of the Household. In K. J. Boudouris, ed., *Ionian Philosophy.* Athens: International Association for Greek Philosophy and International Centre for Greek Philosophy and Culture, pp. 291–7.

O'Meara, O. J. (2014). Iamblichus' *On the Pythagorean Life* in Context. In Huffman 2014a, pp. 399–415.

Pellò, C. (2020a). 'Non solo uomini, ma anche donne … ' La presenza femminile nella filosofia greca e il caso delle pitagoriche. In M. Bonelli, ed., *Filosofe, Maestre, e Imperatrici.* Roma: Edizioni di Storia e Letteratura, pp. 55–78.

Pellò, C. (2020b). Phintys the Pythagorean: A Philosophical Approach. *Philosophia*, 49(2), 11–32.

Pellò, C. (2018). The Lives of Pythagoras: A Proposal for Reading Puythagorean Metempsychosis. *Rhizomata* 6(2), 135–156.

Philip, J. A. (1966). *Pythagoras and Early Pythagoreanism.* Toronto: University of Toronto Press.

Plant, I. M. (2004). *Women Writers of Ancient Greece and Rome.* London: Equinox.

Pomeroy, S. B. (2013). *Pythagorean Women: Their History and Writings.* Baltimore: John Hopkins University Press.

Primavesi, O. (2014). Aristotle on the 'So Called Pythagoreans': From Lore to Science. In Huffman 2014a, pp. 227–49.

Protopapas-Marneli, M. (forthcoming). Cynic Women on Philosophy: The Unique Case of Hipparchia. In K. R. O'Reilly and C. Pellò, eds., *Ancient Women Philosophers*. Cambridge: Cambridge University Press.

Reale, G. (1990). *The Schools of the Imperial Age*. Albany: SUNY Press.

Reeve, C. D. C. (2000). The Naked Old Women in the Palestra. In R. Kraut, ed., *Plato's Republic: Critical Essays*. Lanham: Rowman and Littlefield, pp. 129–41.

Riedweg, C. A. (2015). Pythagoras' Women. *The Classical Review*, 65(1), 96–7.

Riedweg, C. A. (2005). *Pythagoras. His Life, Teaching, and Influence*. Ithaca: Cornell University Press.

Rose, V. (1886), *Aristotelis qui ferebantur librorum fragmenta*. Leipzig: Teubner.

Rostagni, A. (1955–1956). *Scritti Minori*. Torino: Bottega d'Erasmo.

Rowett, C. (2014). The Pythagorean Society and Politics. In Huffman 2014a, pp. 112–30.

Schofield, M. (2012). Pythagoreanism: Emerging from the Presocratic Fog (*Metaphysics* A 5). In C. Steel and O. Primavesi, eds., *Aristotle's Metaphysics Alpha: Symposium Aristotelicum*. Oxford: Oxford University Press, pp. 141–66.

Schorn, S. (2014). Pythagoras in the Historical Tradition: From Herodotus to Diodorus Siculus. In Huffman 2014a, pp. 269–314.

Snyder, J. M. (1991), *The Woman and the Lyre: Women Writers in Classical Greece and Rome*. Carbondale: Southern Illinois University Press.

Snyder, J. M. (1989). *The Woman and The Lyre: Women Writers in Classical Greece and Rome*. Bristol: Bristol Classical.

Städele, A. (1980). *Die Briefe des Pythagoras und der Pythagoreer*. Meisenheim: Hain.

Taylor, J. E. (2006). *Jewish Women Philosophers of First-Century Alexandria*. Oxford: Oxford University Press.

Thesleff, H. (1972). *On the Problem of the Doric Pseudopythagorica*. Åbo: Åbo Akademi.

Thesleff, H. (1965). *The Pythagorean Texts of the Hellenistic Period*. Åbo: Åbo Akademi.

Thesleff, H. (1961). *An Introduction to the Pythagorean Writings of the Hellenistic Period*. Åbo: Åbo Akademi.

Thom, J. C. (2008). The Passions in Neopythagorean Writings. In J. T. Fitzgerald, ed., *Passions and Moral Progress in Greco-Roman Thought*. London: Routledge, pp. 67–78.

References

Twomey, R. (forthcoming). Pythagorean Women and the Running of the Household as a Philosophical Topic. In K. R. O'Reilly and C. Pellò, eds., *Ancient Women Philosophers*. Cambridge: Cambridge University Press.

Ulacco, A. (2917). *Pseudopythagirca Dorica*. Berlin: De Gruyter.

Vítek, T. (2009). The Origins of the Pythagorean *Symbola*. *La Parola del Passato*, 64, 241–70.

Vogel, C. J. (1966). *Pythagoras and Early Pythagoreanism: An Interpretation of Neglected Evidence on the Philosopher Pythagoras*. Assen: Van Grocum.

Waithe, M. E. (1987). *Ancient Women Philosophers, 600 B.C.-500 A.D.* Dordrecht: Springer.

Warren, K. J. (2009). *An Unconventional History of Western Philosophy: Conversations Between Men and Women Philosophers*. Lanham: Rowman and Littlefield.

Wehrli, F. (1974) (ed.). *Die Schule des Aristoteles*. Basel: Schwabe.

Wider, K. (1986). Women Philosophers in the Ancient Greek World: Donning the Mantle. *Hypatia*, 1, 21–62.

Wieland, C. M. (1789). Die Pythagoreischen Frauen. *Historischer Calender für Damen für das Jahr 1790*. Leipzig.

Zhmud, L. (2019). What is Pythagorean of the Pseudopythagorean Literature? *Philologus*, 163(1) 1–23.

Zhmud, L. (2012a). *Pythagoras and the Early Pythagoreans*. Oxford: Oxford University Press.

Zhmud, L. (2012b). Aristoxenus and the Pythagoreans. In Huffman 2012, pp. 223–49.

Acknowledgements

Many thanks to audiences in Durham, Paderborn, Paris, and St Andrews for comments on presentations of this material. Many thanks to Maddalena Bonelli, Gabor Betegh, Giulia de Cesaris, Dorota Dutsch, Constantinos Macris, Katharine O'Reilly, the Footnotes Writing Circle, and the anonymous reviewers for comments on earlier drafts.

Cambridge Elements ≡

Women in the History of Philosophy

Jacqueline Broad
Monash University

Jacqueline Broad is Associate Professor of Philosophy at Monash University, Australia. Her area of expertise is early modern philosophy, with a special focus on 17th- and 18th-century women philosophers. She is the author of *Women Philosophers of the Seventeenth Century* (CUP, 2002); *A History of Women's Political Thought in Europe, 1400–1700* (with Karen Green; CUP, 2009); and *The Philosophy of Mary Astell: An Early Modern Theory of Virtue* (OUP, 2015).

Advisory Board

About the Series
In this Cambridge Elements series, distinguished authors provide concise and structured introductions to a comprehensive range of prominent and lesser-known figures in the history of women's philosophical endeavour, from ancient times to the present day.

Cambridge Elements ☰

Women in the History of Philosophy

Elements in the Series

Printed in the United States
by Baker & Taylor Publisher Services